Actor, Inc.

Actor, Inc.

How to Get the Next Gig—
And Still Pay Your Rent

Jamie Grady

HEINEMANN
Portsmouth, NH

Heinemann
A division of Reed Elsevier Inc.
361 Hanover Street
Portsmouth, NH 03801–3912
www.heinemanndrama.com

Offices and agents throughout the world

Library of Congress Cataloging-in-Publication Data
Grady, Jamie.
    Actor, Inc. : how to get the next gig—and still pay your rent / Jamie Grady.
        p. cm.
    Includes bibliographical references.
    ISBN-13: 978-0-325-01072-4
    ISBN-10: 0-325-01072-2
    1. Acting—Vocational guidance.   I. Title.
PN2055.G66 2007
792.02'8023—dc22   2007024661

Editor: Cheryl Kimball
Production service & typesetting: Kim Arney
Production supervisor: Patricia Adams
Cover design: Joni Doherty Design
Manufacturing: Jamie Carter

Printed in the United States of America on acid-free paper

11   10   09   08   07   VP   1   2   3   4   5

For Kell

![C]ontents

Actor, Inc.

1 Introduction

Why You Should Read This Book

When I first started working in academia, I was asked to teach a course titled Professional Aspects of Theater. The course was created as a means to introduce students to the life of an actor after graduating from college. This task frightened me tremendously. After all, what did I know about being an actor? I had spent the better part of my career in arts administration; I never once auditioned for a role or acted on stage. What was I going to teach these students that they did not already know?

Luckily, there are plenty of good books available about working as a professional actor. Two that come to mind are Brian O'Neil's *Acting as a Business* (1999) and Robert Cohen's *Acting Professionally* (1998). These books cover specifics about training, résumés, auditions, agents, unions, and more. But if students could read a book, why did they need me? In looking at these books, I noticed that they did not cover other important aspects of being an actor. Throughout the semester, I asked working actors to come to class and speak about being actors. Often they ended up talking about money and the strain of living in a major city while pursuing a career in acting.

In reaction to what I was hearing from my guest lecturers, I began to complement the information from these traditional acting books with more general business information that I had learned along the way—things that I wish I had known when I was starting my career in the arts. These areas included time management, personal finances, taxes, and retirement planning. Although the initial reaction from most of the students was one of utter disbelief when I first brought up these subjects, once they completed each assignment, they were grateful for the experience and knowledge.

This book is the result of five years of preparation and research for the Professional Aspects of Theater class and is meant to provide you with a basic business understanding of what you will need to be successful not only as an actor but also as an individual.

We all know that talent is often not enough to launch a successful acting career. As a professional actor, you must be constantly developing as an artist, networking in the field, auditioning, and giving your best work each night you are on stage or in front of the camera. You will make great sacrifices along the way but will also experience rewards not found in the more common professions. Being a professional actor is a unique and demanding lifestyle and career choice.

Each year, thousands of recent college graduates descend upon New York, Los Angeles, and other major cities throughout the country and throughout the world, looking to make it big as actors. Of the 100,000 or more people in the United States who consider themselves professional actors, about 2 to 3 percent of them actually make their living as actors (Cohen 1998, p. 3). Although there are many reasons why people do not fulfill their aspirations to become professional actors, for me the greatest tragedy of all occurs when people with talent, drive, and commitment fall out of the industry, not because they no longer wish to be actors but because they can no longer financially afford the business. They run out of money.

This does not have to happen. If you have the talent and are careful to use your time and money wisely, there should be no reason for you to leave your chosen field due to a lack of resources. This book is designed to get you thinking about your personal and professional life in ways that help you accomplish your goals and become successful as a professional actor, no matter how much money you earn.

Defining Success

Before we proceed any further, let's define *success*. For the purpose of this book, a successful actor is one who can support him- or herself and build a career solely through acting—that 2 to 3 percent of 100,000 actors mentioned earlier. Success is not about being a star or making it big. Success is about maintaining viable employment and sustaining a comfortable living through a career in acting. After all, a professional is one who earns his or her livelihood through a particular field. Being a professional actor is being a success.

We also must remember that being a successful person is not based solely in the career we choose and the accomplishments we reach within that field. Many people commit their lives to helping others by serving a greater good. Are these people as successful as major movie stars? Perhaps so. Other people wish to raise children and be great parents. Are they successful? What about the people who tirelessly work to expose people to the performing arts? Being successful in life is about achieving the goals that you set for yourself. Your life should be a proactive journey that allows you to grow and be successful in many areas of life, not just one aspect.

Success is an individual matter. My definition of success may not be the same as yours. We are not the same people, and we live unique lives. We must think about and ultimately envision our own unique successes. Simply saying that you want to be as successful as certain other people or to have the things they have is not being true to your own self. Sure, someone else's life may look great from the outside, but if it were your life, it might look and feel differently than what you imagine.

To me, being successful is about being happy. Being happy with your life consists of many parts: your job, love, friendships, passions, and family. Ultimately, being happy with what you do brings you success. The great physicist Stephen Hawking is not successful because he thought being a physicist would be a good job and would make him famous. He is successful because he loves science. He had a calling to be a scientist and a thinker, just as you have been called to act and to pursue the arts. Simply by fulfilling your calling you can achieve a level of success. How the rest of the world views your success is unimportant.

Life is a bit of a compromise. Since we never seem to have enough time, money, or energy, we must make choices about how to spend these resources. Buying a new car will limit the purchase of other things. Spending time doing homework will limit time with friends. Life is a balancing act. If you understand this and think about the balances and compromises life presents, you will be able to make better decisions for yourself regarding your personal goals and thus will be successful.

The Idea Behind *Actor, Inc.*

On the first day of class for Professional Aspects of Theater, I ask each student to write his or her name on a piece of paper, add a comma, and then write "Inc." next to that. I tell students this is how they need to think of themselves and their careers from this point forward—as businesses. They must envision themselves not as independent contractors or even as artists but as corporations. It is true that when employed as an actor one earns a salary working for another company, but most acting jobs are short-lived; for example, filming gigs typically last only a few days. Between these jobs an actor might earn a fee through other artistic endeavors such as teaching, earn a salary through a part-time job, or even collect unemployment. An actor's yearly earnings are a combination of many different types of income. As the CEO of your company, you must be constantly looking past the current work at hand and planning the next opportunity, not only for earnings but also for your career's development.

The reality of all this is that an actor's earnings over a given year are rarely consistent and can go from feast to famine in a matter of days. An actor is more like an independent contractor than a salaried employee. Better yet, an actor is more like an entrepreneur—a person who organizes and operates a business and who assumes all of the risks associated with that pursuit. Many of today's best companies were founded by people who possess the same entrepreneurial spirit, who in spite of hardship and setbacks have persevered because of their belief in the work they were doing.

In Thomas J. Stanley and William D. Danko's book *The Millionaire Next Door* (1996), many of their examples of millionaires were entrepreneurs. When you consider it, you might find this not very surprising. As an entrepreneur, your personal and professional livelihood is one and the same. If the business does poorly, so do your personal finances. The two are tied directly. Creating your own company forces you to apply basic business methods to both your career and your personal situation. People who collect a steady and consistent paycheck often do not think much about using their money effectively. They know how to get along on what they have. They tend to live paycheck to paycheck. To earn more money, they need to get a raise or a new job. Successful entrepreneurs, on the other hand, prepare for bad times and plan wisely during healthy times.

The life of an actor follows much of the same path. The difference is that instead of selling physical products or services, actors sell their talents as performers, their artistry. Actors who understand this cultivate the ability to plan, set goals and priorities, and ultimately have an advantage over those actors who fail to fully understand their role as CEOs of their own corporations—themselves.

The principles I use in this book are not special theories only for actors or artists; many of them are fundamental business practices and standard financial investment procedures. They will be easy enough to understand but hard to execute, not because they are difficult to carry out but rather, like maintaining a diet or exercise regime, because people often slip up and fall back on their old ways. Unlike get-rich-quick schemes and easy weight-loss programs, this book requires you to use discipline, planning, and monitoring as you apply the information it contains. However, the rewards will be great. Imagine a life and career where money is no longer an issue. As an artist, the greater your financial autonomy, the greater the risks you can take. Money in the bank ensures artistic freedom.

Additional Contributors

As mentioned earlier, I have never set foot on stage as an actor. Therefore, in order to help complete this book and to add real-world experience and advice, I asked a few professionals to contribute some material. Most of them are actors, but I also asked a financial advisor to add commentary. It has been a pleasure to work with everyone who has contributed to this book. I am humbled and honored by their generosity. I know the book has been made much richer through their insight and wisdom. I have labeled their contributions as Notes from the Field. These real-life examples from people now working in the industry are scattered throughout this book.

As an administrator in theatre and a patron of the arts, I have developed a deep and profound respect for the men and women who have chosen careers as actors. The life of an actor can contain seemingly infinite struggles and sacrifices. Each night when performing on stage, actors expose themselves to an audience of strangers for the benefit of everyone there. Actors tend to travel from town to town, making new friends and leaving them behind once the show is over. Lack of good paying jobs can make this struggle seem meaningless or futile, but successful actors keep their goals in mind. Actors always seem to be moving forward, and the acting life is not so much about getting the next gig as about growth—the process, not the product.

Action Items

At the end of each chapter, I have provided a short list of action items that summarize some of the ways you can take action based on the chapter's discussion. You should complete these items before moving on to the next chapter's items. It is not necessary to stop reading the book while you complete these items, but I do recommend that you complete the action items in order, from one chapter to the next. I have organized the information in a linear fashion according to standard business/personal planning processes. Even though you may read ahead prior to completing certain action items, please try to follow the action items in order. If you do so, I believe you will enjoy the book more thoroughly.

You may also find the action items useful when reviewing chapter information. Business/personal planning is the culmination of planning, implementation, and evaluation actions that are simultaneously taking place. It is about formulating plans and strategies for action, implementing those actions, and evaluating those actions to determine whether planning goals have been met. Sounds simple enough, but this process will require knowledge and discipline. After moving through certain exercises or tasks, you may find it useful to reread chapters or sections to evaluate your effectiveness. This is not a one-time fix; it is a constant, unending process.

Here are the action items for this chapter.

- On a piece of paper, do the following.
  - Write your name.
  - Add a comma after your name.
  - Add "Inc" after that
  Congratulations—you are now a business!
- Begin to define your individual meaning of success.

2 The Artistic Entrepreneur

The Home Office

Let's face facts. Being a professional actor requires both art and commerce. You probably know a lot about the art of being an actor but less about the business of being one. Actors have rehearsal halls, studios, and theatres in which to practice, rehearse, and perform their artistry, but do you have an office where you conduct your business? If you were running a company or working as an employee, you would expect to have a desk, a phone, a fax machine, a computer, and other things you would need to conduct your daily affairs in a professional manner. Then why don't you have a space designated for your acting business? Not having these tools readily available costs you time, money, and opportunities.

Setting up a home office is an important first step in the management of your career. A home office provides you with the tools necessary to be successful. No matter what your style, having a place to file papers and organize your professional life will pay off. After all, organization is a prized managerial trait, and having an office will help you become more organized. Organization makes you more effective and efficient. In the end, you will get more done in less time.

When you think of a home office, you might envision having all the latest communication gadgets, computers, large filing cabinets, and a big desk on which to stretch out your feet. But if you are living in a major city in a small apartment, this type of setup is not very realistic or practical. When planning for your home office, consider those things that are essential. You will need a phone, which could be a cell phone (if you have good reception in your home); you will need a filing system to hold important papers, pay stubs, information on contacts, reviews, and other useful reference materials. You will probably need a fax machine to get scripts and sides, and it would probably serve you well to have a computer, a printer, and Internet capabilities.

Now think about the activities you might do in your home office: sending out mailings, making phone calls, hunting for jobs, planning for the future. What things might you need for these activities? What is your personal style? Are you a technology junkie who enjoys using the latest office tools, or do you prefer the old ways of pencil and paper? The answers to these questions will help you determine what you will need in your office. It is your space—it should reflect your work style.

As for the physical space of your office, you may use a small table or desk in your living room (if it is quiet) or in your bedroom. Try to partition off the space from the rest of the room in some manner. This could mean using a small rug, hanging a cloth from the ceiling to divide the space, or creating some other physical characteristic that tells you this is a place for work. When you enter the space, you should know that you came to this place to conduct business; it is different from the rest of your living space. This place should also be respected in the sense that it should not be a place to drape dirty clothes or dump unwanted mail. Keep the space clear and ready for use. These might seem silly suggestions, but they set up a way of thinking that your work life needs to be respected and taken care of in a different way than your daily personal life.

In your home office, you want to gather all the materials you need to run your business. Your office is the place where you store your headshots, cover letters, and demos. It is where you keep copies of *Back Stage* and the *Ross Reports* as well as reviews of your work. This is the place to keep all of your records about your contacts, including when you last spoke with them and what actions were taken. Just as if you were working in an office across town, you need to gather all the resources necessary to make your work efficient and effective.

Finally, objectively consider your email address, blog site, My-Space account, and answering machine message. Are they professional? Do they communicate to potential clients the kind of image you wish to convey? If not, you need to change them immediately. Email addresses and answering machine messages are part of your outward appearance to the business world. While you might think your current choices are cute or clever, someone else might think otherwise. Search for your name on Google, and see what you get. Do the results portray you as a professional actor? If not, change them. It might be a valuable use of your time and energy deleting or cleaning up your blogs, personal pages, or websites that may lead to a poor first impression. More and more employers use the Internet to search for information on potential employees. You need to be careful. What may have seemed like fun to post for your college friends to read may say something completely different to other people. In all of your activities, try to maintain a high level of professionalism. Don't let people judge you by a faulty outside appearance—let them judge you by the quality of your auditions and work.

Notes from the Field: The Whole Desk Thing

Having an office is very important! Since I have lived in New York City, I have been lucky to have roommates who had computers and who didn't mind that I used them. By using them, I not only checked my email but also did electronic casting submissions. This is a great way to send out your stuff because it's faster, and you don't have to spend money on stamps, manila envelopes, or more and more headshots. Reprints cost money: 100 copies usually go for $100. There are other options, such as creating lithographs and getting copies from an online company. It depends on what you feel comfortable doing.

Using my roommates' computers meant I kept my résumé and my headshots on their computers. This took up space on their computers and brought up questions about what to do if we needed to use the same computer at the same time. The other problem was that my roommates didn't have a printer, so I had to go to computer printing shops and download my résumé, print it out, and cut it into the 8 × 10 size. I always tried to make a lot of copies at one time so that I did not have to keep going back to the shop, but printing extra copies meant I spent more money.

The best thing I ever did was:

- Get a laptop. (It travels better.)
- Get a printer. (I can just print my résumé when I need it. I can change it when I need to and not have extra copies of a résumé I don't use.)

I have moved into a loft, so I do have more space now. Having an open space, I have made office walls with my bookshelves and a fish tank. However, I do not have my desk yet! My kitchen table is big enough that it acts as my desk for now, but I have been procrastinating because I want an old-fashioned desk. I am getting a little tired myself. I have all these boxes with my paperwork, headshots, *Ross Reports*, scripts. I just have to get a desk with all the drawers I need and get the business a little more organized. I will feel like I am actually a business if my space is more defined and I'm not working at my kitchen table so much. My boyfriend is a painter, and he has his studio in the loft. We put up some walls and a screen, and he goes into his studio/office and works on his paintings. It seems more real, even more important in some ways.

—P. H.

MySpace and Other Social Network Sites

A new business tool has been given to actors through the recent rise of social network sites such as MySpace, Facebook, and Friendster. If you went to college, you probably know these sites can be great tools for meeting people and socializing with them prior to face-to-face meetings or dates. These sites can also be used to keep up with friends and family by posting information to share with everyone in your group. While many people use such sites for personal experiences, businesses, particularly entertainment companies, are using these sites as marketing tools to sell their products. Actors can learn a lesson from these groups and adapt their strategies to develop sites that help promote their own careers.

Again, the balance is between professional and personal use. Expect people to visit your MySpace page. If I were a casting director or a director, what would I see? Would I see someone who is put together, organized, confident, and professional, or would I see otherwise? Appearances are important, especially in the acting business.

A social network site can be a great place to develop a fan page. For example, you could provide a number of headshots, photos from past productions, reviews from newspapers, and links to the companies you worked with. A fan page is also a good way to let people know what you are doing next. Self-promotion is part of the business. It is not just about encouraging casting directors to hire you—it is also about developing a fan base for your work.

As you begin to develop your career as an actor, consider the tools that technology has given you to make yourself more visible to the people in the business. Recognize that using such technology requires a certain amount of responsibility to keep a professional appearance at all times. Also remember that these sites require constant maintenance and upkeep, so be careful of doing too much. Keep your site simple and professional.

A Business Plan for Actors

The point of creating an office space, as well as the point of this book, is to create a paradigm shift that changes your assumptions and beliefs about acting from those of a career of random happenstance to those of a career thoughtfully planned and implemented. Organizing a cluttered collection of papers into an office space is the first step of this shift. The next step is planning.

When creating a business, the entrepreneur usually writes a business plan to show to banks or other potential investors as a means to raise the funds necessary to begin operation. The business plan outlines the manner in which the business will be run: the who, what, why, and where. Since the business plan typically documents the short- and long-term goals of the business, it can also be used as a benchmark against actual performance. A business plan begins to establish goals and objectives for the company in the short term. In many ways, business planning is a lot like personal time management, which we'll examine in Chapter 3.

During this planning process, the entrepreneur conducts a SWOT analysis. SWOT stands for strengths, weaknesses, opportunities, and threats. Strengths and weaknesses are internal factors, while opportunities and threats are part of the external environment. Going through the process of a SWOT analysis is an attempt to take an objective look at the company and the world around it. For an actor, particular strengths might be the ability to sing, dance, or speak a foreign language. Strengths are all of those things you might put on your acting résumé. Weaknesses might be the opposite: the inability to carry a tune, dance, or speak a second language. At times, your greatest strength could be your greatest weakness. For example, you might have a particularly strong résumé for Shakespearean acting, which is great for getting auditions for Elizabethan plays but not very good for getting auditions for musicals.

Opportunities and threats are part of the environment, such as the types of plays and films that are hot in the market, the number of theatres in your area, and the general state of the industry itself (e.g., current strikes, layoffs, and so on). These are all important considerations as you begin and continue in your career. Although we cannot always control the environment we live in, we can adjust our behavior to prepare for threats or to position ourselves for potential opportunities. In some situations, we may have to relocate to best facilitate our career. For example, many actors choose between New York and Los Angeles not because of weather but because New York is more supportive of a theatre career, whereas Los Angeles is more supportive of a career in television and film.

As an actor, it is important for you to understand and recognize your strengths and weaknesses and how they come together with the opportunities and threats of the field. If you are a film actor living in New York, you may be limiting your opportunities for work. Through the SWOT exercise, you want to determine what you do particularly well, what makes you unique and distinctive. Some actors and artists might call this determining your type. You want to clarify where in the field your talents and distinctiveness best fit and where the best opportunities lie.

In evaluating your weaknesses as an actor, you might consider comments heard in the past regarding why you did not get certain parts or reviews of shows that you were in. Were you described as

hard to hear or heavy on your feet? You might focus on these areas to improve certain skills. When weaknesses are identified, you
should take reasonable action to correct them. You might take
dancing or singing lessons or enroll in a classical acting program.
The more talent you develop, the more marketable you are to the
industry. However, not every actor has the ability to be a triple
threat, nor do the directors of the world want every actor to have
the same skill set. If this were the case, the stage and screen would
be pretty boring places.

In fact, it might not be in your best interest to try to improve
certain inadequacies; rather, you might benefit more by capitaliz-
ing on and expanding your strengths—again, another paradigm
shift. In the article "Managing Oneself" published in the *Harvard
Business Review*, Peter Drucker states, "Success . . . comes to those
who know themselves—their strengths, their values, and how
they best perform" (Drucker 2005, pp. 100–07). In this fascinat-
ing article, Drucker asks his readers to consider the following:

- What are my strengths?
- How do I perform?
- What are my values?
- Where do I belong?
- What should I contribute?
- What is my responsibility for relationships?

Instead of focusing on areas of weakness, Drucker says we
should focus on our individual strengths and put ourselves in situations where those strengths can produce the greatest results.
Conversely, we should not let ourselves get into situations where
we cannot be successful. Drucker states that we should work on
improving our skills, building upon what we have and increasing
our expertise.

In other words, instead of being a well-rounded actor competent in several areas, focus on your particular strengths and become better or even great in those areas. What particular talent
sets you apart from all the rest? How can you increase the dis-
tance between your skills and those of other actors? For example,
if you are naturally funny, you might consider building those
skills by enrolling in comedic classes. For inspiration, think of

current examples of people already in the field who have capital-ized on their particular strengths as performers.

Take a moment now to conduct a SWOT analysis on your life and career. Get out a piece of paper. As objectively as you can, an-swer these questions: What are your strengths and weaknesses as an actor and a performer? In your current environment, where are there opportunities for an actor of your ability? What are the threats and challenges within that environment? You can best see this information by placing it in a matrix like the one shown in Figure 2–1.

Having taken a hard look at yourself and the world around you, you can begin to make plans for the future. At this point, you should have a better understanding of the things you need to do to improve your chances of becoming a successful professional actor. Ask yourself some more questions: How can your particular strengths lead you to greater opportunities and a more stable ca-reer? Which of your weaknesses can you fix or do you wish to fix? What threats in the environment affect your career potential, and how might you correct that situation? What are your priori-ties in your career?

Having listed your strengths, weaknesses, opportunities, and threats, you can begin to consider your short- and long-term goals. What things can you manage in the short term? What things will take time (two to three years) to complete? Breaking down goals in this manner will make them more manageable when thinking about goals and when taking action to achieve them. Chapter 3 will explore how to create short- and long-term goals and how to manage your time to successfully reach your goals.

Strengths	Weaknesses
Internal/Positive	Internal/Negative
Opportunities	**Threats**
External/Positive	External/Negative

Figure 2–1. SWOT Matrix

Notes from the Field: Thinking About Your Career as a Business

They definitely did not teach me to think of my career as a business when I left school with my Bachelor of Science in Theatre. I walked out having done some good shows, lived in London studying Shakespeare, and learned some technical aspects of theatre, and I knew I wanted to work as an actor. I moved to Los Angeles when I graduated, and I thought the people there would care about me. Well, I thought they would at least want to meet me. Los Angeles is all business. It's Hollywood. I guess I thought this meant lots of parties and sunshine and we'd all be making movies. I was coming from this artistic heaven of a liberal arts college in the Northeast, where I had just done a production of Thorton Wilder's *The Skin of Our Teeth*. Didn't they want to hear all about it?

Meanwhile, I injured my voice, got nodules at the end of my senior year at college (from partying too much and doing shows; I did a children's musical for six months in Santa Monica), and I started working with a big-time voice teacher. We had a great relationship, and he started sending me out on singing auditions for new girl groups and to a producer looking for the lead vocalist for a band. I made a demo that I was very happy with, and so was my teacher. The feedback I got from my vocal coach was that my voice was exactly what the producer was looking for, but I wasn't thin enough and didn't have enough of an image.

They want to completely label you as soon as possible because you have to give people something they recognize. The first acting school I went to in Los Angeles was very highly recommended because a lot of famous actors had studied there. I was very excited, but I had never experienced what happened to me on the first day of class. I had to sit on stage, in front of all eighty students, and they looked at me and decided whom I looked like, and then from there I would work on scenes from their movies.

This is very important to learn. I don't think I would ever recommend doing it that way, but knowing who you are can only make it easier on you when you are trying to get work. I'm not the blond bombshell. What kind of films/TV do I want to do? Who are the actors I like? Am I similar to any of them? Could I also play one of their roles? If I want to do theatre, is Los Angeles the right place for me? I would never take back going out to Los Angeles and really seeing what that is. I know I still want to be part of that, but when I have a job.

I learned Los Angeles is Hollywood, which means that is all business. If they don't know who you are, how can they make money off you? Could they release a film starring you, and would people come see it? Would you pay back the millions of dollars they spent to make the movie?

I needed a little release from it all. That's why I moved to New York City and chose to study with William Esper at his studio, learning the Meisner technique for two years. I just needed to focus on my craft. Now I'm out, and I have to get my business head on. The business of acting I'm still learning. I feel like I constantly have to remind myself that acting is a business. It does not have to be if I want to keep it as a hobby. I don't work in a restaurant, babysit, and live month to month for a hobby, but I want to act, so that is what I have to do.

I have found you have to start really seeing yourself in a business way. I have to change my way of thinking. I have to see myself as a product that people would want to sell and that people are going to buy. When I have gone out on some meetings with agents, they have asked me, "Who do you see yourself like?" In New York, they ask these questions, too. It doesn't matter what city you are in—the business is the business. I had my answer, and some people really agreed, but others had different suggestions. I learned a lot from that. You never know what other people see in you. We played a game at my restaurant job about who would play everyone who worked there if someone made a movie based on this restaurant. For my part, people chose Sarah Jessica Parker (which I get on a regular basis) acting with the intensity of Brittany Murphy in *Girl, Interrupted*. I was really excited about this because I learned something new about myself, and I also see this as a selling point for the business side of acting. I do have this darker kind of crazed, overwhelmed side to myself. I would love to play manic women. Agents would understand this. It's a certain language they use; they could sell me with this description to casting directors. I find myself describing people in this way because that is what people know. Not just agents, but people who watch movies and live with pop culture surrounding them.

—P. H.

Action Items

- Create a home office space for your business.
- Gather the necessary paperwork and resources needed to conduct your business:
  - Headshots, résumés, and demos
  - Publications
  - Contact information
  - Press clippings
- Procure the necessary equipment to do your job efficiently and effectively. (Save the receipts!)
- Conduct your own SWOT analysis.
- Break out the results of your SWOT analysis into short- and long-term goals.

3 The Principles of Time Management

Three of the Seven Habits

When most people think of time management, they immediately think of calendars and schedules, appointments and deadlines. They think of time restrictions instead of what proper time management can do: create more available time. Time management and personal planning are about preparing for opportunities, trying to put yourself in situations where you can be the most successful. "Successful careers are not planned. They develop when people are prepared for opportunities" (Drucker 2005, p. 106). Time management allows people to take control of their lives and to organize themselves around what is important to them—their own goals. Moving your career methodically from one step to another, from one opportunity to the next, will help create focus and meaning. Planning gives people direction and the tools to achieve their goals.

In Stephen Covey's book *The Seven Habits of Highly Effective People* (1989), the first three habits—Be Proactive, Begin with the End in Mind, and Put First Things First—are to me the most important. They are the basis of time management (as well as business planning). *Be Proactive* speaks for itself: Nothing is going to come to you, so you need to make things happen for yourself. You do this not by reacting to the environment but rather by being proactive. Being proactive "means more than merely taking initiative. It means that as human beings, we are responsible for our own lives. Our behavior is a function of our decisions, not our conditions. We have initiative and the responsibility to make things happen" (Covey 1989, p. 71). As an artistic entrepreneur, you have the sole responsibility of making your career happen. Certainly, there will be times when you feel at the mercy of others to help your career, to hire you for the part or cast you in a show, but there are countless ways to make opportunities happen on your own.

The second habit, *Begin with the End in Mind*, is important as a means to recognize our personal goals and aspirations. In this section of his book, Covey asks the reader to create a personal mission statement. In a slightly morbid exercise, he asks you to imagine your own funeral. He asks you to visualize the people in attendance and then, as each person comes up to speak about a particular aspect of your life, he asks you to listen to what they are saying. What you have them say will ultimately be what you seek to aspire to. Your family, friends, coworkers, and community will be speaking about you; what will you have them say? Before your career ends, what do you wish to accomplish as an actor? Do you always want to be an actor, or is this a jumping-off point to another career? How do you define success both on and off the stage? Creating a personal mission statement "focuses on what you want to be (character) and to do (contributions and achievements) and on the values or principles upon which being and doing are based" (Covey 1989, p. 106). As the great exchange goes between Alice and the Cheshire cat in *Alice's Adventures in Wonderland*:

> "Would you tell me, please, which way I ought to go from here?"
> "That depends a good deal on where you want to get to," said the Cat.
> "I don't much care where—" said Alice.
> "Then it doesn't matter which way you go," said the Cat.
> (Carroll 1980, pp. 79–80)

The idea here is to know where you are going and to make sure you are on the right road to get there.

In a way, you began this process in Chapter 2 when you conducted your SWOT analysis in terms of your career. Now you are being asked to combine your professional goals with your personal goals. It is difficult for most people to separate their personal and professional lives. In the arts, it is even more difficult because our life's passion is our vocation. For this reason, it is crucial that you become aware of not only your professional ambitions but also your life's ambitions. Becoming a successful actor may not be as fulfilling as you may have hoped, especially if you sacrifice too much of yourself along the way. In this exercise, we can begin to find a balance between the two.

Try the funeral exercise for yourself. Who comes up to the podium to speak on behalf of your life: partners, children, grandchildren, actors, directors, community members, friends, all the people who are part of a rich life? What do they say about you: your spirit, drive, generosity, humor, way of life, accomplishments? It may seem like a fantasy, but this *is* your dream life. It makes sense to try to understand what you are seeking to accomplish in life. These are your goals in life. Write down these goals and aspirations, and write your personal mission statement. In each of the roles of your life, how do you want to live and be remembered? What things do you value in life? As your ambitions become clearer to you, it will become more important for you to find the time and energy to make them a reality.

A Personal Mission Statement Defined

For a business, a mission statement is "a single sentence or short paragraph that states the company's central philosophy, beliefs, values, and principles. It is a simple expression of why an organization was created and what it will accomplish" (Grady 2006, p. 6). Unfortunately, for this particular exercise human beings are a bit more complex than companies. People generally have three areas of focus: personal, professional, and community/social. And for each of these areas, we hold our own sets of goals and desires. Creating a single sentence for all of these would be virtually impossible. Therefore, it is my recommendation, as Covey suggests in *The Seven Habits of Highly Effective People*, to begin by listing each of your current and future roles: son/daughter, brother/sister, partner, father/mother, actor, advocate, friend, neighbor, and so on. Then try to create a single sentence that encapsulates all of what you have listed. These exercises will get you thinking about the type of person you wish to become and will prepare you for plotting a strategy for your success. My personal mission and vision statements appear on the next page.

My Personal Mission Statement

To live life to the fullest through those experiences that bring love, happiness, enrichment, and wisdom

To achieve my mission, I will seek:

- to always do my best
- to express my love to those who mean most to me
- to keep family first
- to live life with integrity, honesty, love, and laughter
- to live life modestly, without sacrificing comfort or quality
- to be wise with my money, having it work for me rather than against me
- to live life without fear—we are all the same and all afraid
- to not take anything personally and to not make assumptions
- to seek artistic fulfillment through practice and participation
- to find time for friends
- to listen more than I speak
- to be loyal to those who are not around

My Personal Vision Statement

To be secure emotionally, spiritually, physically, and financially

Of course, this is just one example. I suggest going to the FranklinCovey website at www.franklincovey.com and trying the Mission Statement Builder. I recommend using the Mission Kickstart as a good way to start thinking about your values. The site also contains some inspirational quotes that might help motivate you into action.

Once you have created your personal mission statement, read through it a few times. Try to memorize its core values. Then put your mission statement in a place that is easily accessible or, better yet, visible, so that you may reference it whenever you make plans in the future.

Focus on the Things That Matter Most

The German poet, novelist, playwright, courtier, and natural philosopher Johann Wolfgang von Goethe said it best: "things which matter most must never be at the mercy of things which matter least." In a world of constant connections and distractions, it is a wonder we get anything meaningful done at all. Think back on an average day. How much time did you spend talking on the phone, returning emails, searching the Internet, playing video games, or watching television? Now think about how much of those activities were important to you. *What important things did you not get done?*

Each and every one of us is a unique combination of personal values and principles; effective people organize and act based on their own priorities. Your priorities are determined by your personal mission statement, your character, and your pursuit of individual achievements and contributions. "Prioritizing means determining the relative importance and precedence of events. And it is absolutely necessary for effective planning. Prioritizing keeps us from spending time on things we don't value. It prevents the most important events in our lives from being victimized by less important activities" (Smith 1995, p. 103). In a world of constant information and interruptions, it takes determination to keep our priorities in focus.

The principles of a mission statement and priorities are also a part of business life. The leaders of a corporation are responsible for determining the organization's direction and vision. The leaders, through the mission and vision statements, determine the organization's priorities, those things that will make it possible for the company to reach its future desired state. Managers are responsible for making the top priorities part of the day-to-day life of the organization. In your organization, you are both the leader and the manager. You will set the long-range goals as well as implement them each day.

Notes from the Field: Paying Your Dues

It's easy to get caught up in the idea that, as a professional artist trained and educated for your vocation, you should hold out for only the paying gigs—and then accept only the ones that pay at a rate comparable to gigs you've done previously or the ones with a theatre/production company that will provide you a union card or elevate

continued

your status as an actor. My suggestion is, while you aren't restricted by union mandates, to strongly consider auditioning for and taking *every* gig you're able to schedule, and make the paycheck the last concern. Of course, there are things to consider: Is it a good role for you? Will it be a challenge? Will it help flesh out your résumé? Is there any chance you'll be able to network with other actors and artistic, managing, or production staffers? Is the rehearsal/production schedule reasonable and workable around your day job? Will there be other compensation, such as free tickets for agents and casting directors— or, in the case of film/video/voiceover work, will you receive a DVD or CD of the finished product?

You may be concerned about a bigger potential casting opportunity that might come up while you're busy with the less sexy job. Having been on both sides of casting, I can say that it's much more impressive to those who might like to hire you that you're unavailable because you're busy with a project than if you're sitting by the phone wishing for the perfect job to come along. It's the old proverb: A bird in the hand is worth more than two in the bush. Most of the time casting directors don't know that what you're doing is small potatoes (particularly if you don't talk of it as such), and if you're really whom they want, they'll most likely try to work around your commitment.

So, say that a small-potato gig comes along, you're available, and it sounds like an interesting project. What if the word on the street is that the director is difficult to work with, or the theatre/production company has produced a turkey or two or is lame in some other way? Will it be worse for your career to be associated with one of their productions than to do nothing? You certainly want to consider the reputation of those with whom you're getting involved, but also be sure to consider what the source of such a rumor might be: Often sour grapes are propagated by actors or other artists who weren't hired or had difficulties with the company/artistic staff because of their own shortcomings. If you're professional, pleasant, prompt, affable, adaptable, and, above all, reliable, the potential of making contacts for future opportunities far outweighs the risks of soiling your reputation. Moreover, much of the most exciting theatre and film work ever done was spawned in small, low-budget, independent companies. If you *do* end up in a stinker of a show, try to consider it as a learning experience that seasons your capability to work positively in a difficult situation. This is what they call *paying your dues*. Think of how many Hollywood stars have been in a turkey of a film and still gone on to fame in bigger and better things.

—K. S.

A Time Management Exercise

Proper time management is more than setting priorities and carrying them out. Life is a myriad of activities and responsibilities, ranging in scale from mundane to life changing. For this reason, many successful people use personal day planners, personal digital assistants (PDAs), and other tools to help plan their lives. Proper time management merges short- and long-term priorities with the day-to-day commitments of life. Your long-term goals should not be at the mercy of trivial day-to-day activities. If you had the time to focus on your long-term goals, what would you be doing?

Although different time management systems work best for different people, I encourage you to begin with the method described in this section and then adapt it to what you have learned and what works best for you. However, it is important that you stick with the system described for a least one month in order to truly understand and appreciate its benefits.

To begin, you will need to purchase or create a one-month calendar/planner (save the receipt). The calendar should contain one page with the entire month on it. Then you will need to find refills with *one day on two pages*. I personally use the Day-Timer refills, but FranklinCovey and Day Runner have very similar products. I prefer the Day-Timer system because the appointments section runs from 7:00 A.M. to 10:00 P.M.; the others stop at 8:00 P.M.

Another cheaper method to try is using an online calendar program, such as Google (www.google.com) or Yahoo! (www.yahoo.com). I suggest, however, not to use them like a PDA but rather to enter all of your information, print it all, and put the printed pages into a binder so that you will always have access.

Always have your calendar with you so that when you need to add appointments or check availability, you know your schedule exactly. No more guesswork.

Step 1: Create a Master To-Do List

At one time or another, all of us have gotten so frustrated with everything we had to do that we decided to sit down and write it all out. We created a to-do list. As we moved through each task, we crossed it off the list or put a check next to it to remind us of our accomplishments. And it made us feel good every time we did it. The act of crossing a task off the list made us want to do more. It made us feel like we were accomplishing things. Personal planning works in very much the same way, but even better.

With your personal mission statement in mind, begin to list all the things that you would like to do in life. Maybe you want to travel, enroll in a cooking class, or get new headshots. Try to consider all of your values and priorities. In other words, think about your immediate goals and aspirations, but do not be afraid to dream big. If you have large goals, break them into smaller objectives. Perhaps you have not researched headshot photographers or you need to save money for the cooking class. These steps become objectives for reaching your goals. In this way, you break your goals into more workable action steps. For example, getting new headshots would break down into the following tasks.

- Ask friends about their experiences with photographers.
- Save money for a session and reproductions.
- Conduct online research of photographers, prices, and packages.
- Meet with at least four photographers to find one you want to work with.
- Set up an appointment.
- Go to the appointment!
- Get information on reproductions.
- Have reproductions made.

Do this for all of your goals and aspirations, breaking them into smaller, more achievable objectives. Make sure to include all the aspects of your life, not just your career goals. You will need to have fun, too. I imagine that your list will be pretty long.

Finally, you should include the more routine aspects of life: shopping for groceries, picking up the dry cleaning, returning phone calls. These things might be weighing on your mind right now. These might be urgent activities that need your attention very soon.

The list of all your upcoming tasks is your master to-do list. If possible, store this list on a computer for future reference. That way, as you accomplish tasks and add new ones, you don't have to keep rewriting your list. Although if you're one of those people who likes to write everything out, go ahead and rewrite your list by hand—whatever works best for you.

Step 2: Prioritize Your To-Do List

Now that you have this monstrous list of things to do, how do you go about accomplishing what is on the list? When faced with such a list, many people might simply throw it away (too much to do!) or just start from the top and work their way down the list. But if you prioritize the items on the list, you will know what needs to be done first and what can wait for later. This is what you will do in this step.

Most planning systems use the A, B, C + 1, 2, 3 method of prioritizing goals and objectives. I like to think of the A, B, and C priorities this way:

A = very important, high value, to be done immediately

B = important, moderate value, to be done soon

C = somewhat important, low value or optional, to be done later

The timing of when a certain activity needs to be completed or its value to you in relationship to your personal mission statement will dictate whether the item gets an A, a B, or a C. You would not have written down the activity if it was not important, but its importance, as with all things, may change over time. For example, an A-priority task might be to save money for a C-priority trip. However, as you begin to save, the C item will move up to a B priority, and after you plan your trip, it will be an A priority: Go on a trip to London!

Here's what the numbers in this method signify:

1 = must be done in the next twenty-four to forty-eight hours

2 = must be done soon

3 = can be put off in order to do more important activities

So let's say you need to go grocery shopping soon; you are running low on milk. Today, grocery shopping might be an A3 on your list, tomorrow an A2, and when you run out of food, grocery shopping becomes an A1 priority, something that must get done today.

Look through your master to-do list, and begin assigning each goal or activity a letter value (A, B, or C). Here is where a bit of reality must enter the picture. Earlier I asked you to dream; now I am asking you not to forget your dreams but to be a bit more realistic about what you can accomplish in the next six to nine months. Like any business, your two most precious resources are time and money. Leaders of organizations typically allocate these resources to the two to four most important goals, the ones that have the greatest potentials of advancing the company to its vision—in your case, that vision is to become a professional actor. This means that some of your goals may have to wait. For example, let's say you have five major (high-value) goals in mind:

- Attend graduate school.
- Take singing lessons.
- Travel to Italy.
- Find an agent.
- Get a new job.

All of these goals fit into your personal mission statement, but all of them in one way or another require time and money. Thinking through your list, you realize that getting a new job has to be your first priority. Without a new, higher-paying job, you cannot afford the rest of the goals, nor could you realistically plan for them. Therefore, getting a new job becomes an A priority for you. Through the work you have done with your SWOT analysis, you feel that taking singing lessons is probably your next-highest goal, as strengthening your vocal ability will open you up to more roles and therefore will make you more appealing to an agent. This, too, becomes an A priority. For now you decide to focus on these two priorities before going any further with the other three. After all, if you improve your singing and get an agent, graduate school would wait; conversely, if you have trouble finding an agent, graduate school might become a better option. But you feel that you would like to make an earnest attempt at signing with an agent before you consider graduate school. A trip to Italy will have to wait until your career begins to strengthen. Your new, prioritized list of goals might look something like this:

A—Get a new job.

A—Take singing lessons.

B—Find an agent.

C—Attend graduate school.

C—Travel to Italy.

Reducing the number of A priorities on your list will provide you with the focus you need to obtain those goals. Again, break these goals into more manageable objectives or action items, such as create a new business résumé, go to the library and look through the help wanted section of the paper, ask friends about their experiences with vocal coaches, and so on.

At this point in time, you should have a pretty reasonable list of things to do to move you toward your goals, and you should be focused on own your main priorities for the next six months to a year. After all, you can't expect to sing well after one singing lesson. Progress will take time.

Do not forget that you still have to plan for all the little things in life as well! Add to your to-do list all the day-to-day things that you need to get done: dry cleaning, birthday cards, hair appointments. Assign these action items both letter and number priorities. On the master to-do list, I like to think of numbers representing weeks: A1 = things to do this week, A2 = things to do next week, and A3 = things to be done the third week. I typically do not number B or C priorities on the master to-do list. Again, you will find a system that works for you.

An Example of a Master To-Do List

A1—Look through help wanted ads for a new job. (*Get a new job.*)

A1—Prepare a new business/nonacting *résumé*. (*Get a new job.*)

A1—Look into temp service work. (*Get a new job.*)

A1—Ask around about a vocal coach. (*Take singing lessons.*)

A1—Save money to pay for singing lessons. (*Take singing lessons.*)

A2—Pick up dry cleaning.

A2—Pay bills.

A3—Buy printer paper for home office.

B—Call my parents.

B—Call Diane about the party.

B—Get a haircut.

B—Ask around about people's agents. (*Find an agent.*)

C—Start searching for possible grad schools. (*Attend graduate school.*)

C—Pick up information about a trip to Italy. (*Travel to Italy.*)

Your own list will probably be much larger than this example. My master to-do list usually runs about one to two pages long, typically hovering around a page and a half. This list contains many types of activities, ranging from important things that must be done immediately to other things that serve more as reminders about goals I wish to achieve. The great thing about this list is it is a place where I can review all of my objectives as well as include new ones as I move through the workweek.

Having a basic to-do list is pretty common among people trying to get an understanding of what they need to do, but prioritizing the list is less common. Applying that list to a calendar system is even less common. This is our next step.

Step 3: Set Up Your Monthly Calendar

The monthly calendar will be your primary source of information when planning your activities (Figure 3–1). On your calendar page, you should list all your appointments, work shifts, and regularly scheduled activities (e.g., going to the gym each morning at 7:00 A.M.). You should also block out vacations, parties, and other social obligations. Any activity that you are currently committed to should be placed on the monthly calendar. This way, when you need to schedule a meeting or another activity, everything is there for you to see. Since schedules and meetings change, you should write everything in pencil and try to develop a shorthand system that works for you.

Sun	Mon	Tues	Wed	Thurs	Fri	Sat
			1 7 Gym 9–3 Wk	2 11–5 Wk	3 7 Gym 5–cls Wk	4 11–5 Wk
5	6 7 Gym	7 9–3 Wk	8 7 Gym 9–3 Wk	9 11–5 Wk	10 7 Gym DER's Prty	11 11–5 Wk 5–cls Wk
12	13 7 Gym 2 Ph intrv.	14 9–3 Wk	15 7 Gym 9–3 Wk	16 11–5 Wk	17 7 Gym 11 Mtg. w/Agent 5–cls Wk	18 11–5 Wk
19 2 Matinee	20 7 Gym Calls for trip	21 9–3 Wk 4 Tom S. Apt.	22 7 Gym 9–3 Wk	23 11–5 Wk	24 7 Gym 5–cls Wk	25 11–5 Wk Out of town
26 Out of town	27 Out of town	28 9–3 Wk	29 7 Gym 9–3 Wk	30 11–5 Wk		

Figure 3–1   Sample Monthly Calendar

The example shown in Figure 3–1 includes regular activities of going to the gym three days a week as well as a steady but varying work schedule. It also includes personal appointments, such as a party on the 10th and tickets to see a show on the 19th. This person has also planned a trip out of town on the 25th through the 27th. You can see how easy it will be for this person to schedule other activities since the calendar shows exactly what has been scheduled already.

Let us imagine for a moment that this person was booked for a show with rehearsals starting in a week. This actor would know by looking at the calendar what previous appointments would need to change to accommodate rehearsals and what exactly would need to be done when. If this person uses the monthly calendar properly, there will be no surprise meetings or appointments.

The benefit of a monthly calendar is that it provides you with a view of all your obligations with one look. As your monthly commitments develop, you can take charge of your time in many positive ways. For example, you may want to give yourself a day off from everything and catch up on some sleep, so you put a line through the Tuesday two weeks from now and keep new appointments off that day. If you are already going downtown on Friday for an appointment, you may try to schedule another meeting with someone else near the same location a little later that day, saving you time, money, and a bit of running around. Or you may want to stop by the store around the corner to pick up the birthday gift for your friend so you can cross that task off your master to-do list. A monthly calendar system moves you out of planning one day at a time and lets you look at your life in bigger blocks of time. This gives you better control of your day, week, month, and ultimately life.

For example, I like to do paperwork and teach class in the morning, so I try to keep meetings relegated to afternoon times. I also try to do as much as I can during the beginning of the week, so Fridays are light days. That's my style. Through this system, you can develop your own style and find what works best for you.

Many people who use personal calendars to help organize their lives use daily or weekly calendars. When a person using a daily calendar opens a page, he or she comes across all the work and appointments scheduled for a particular day without knowing how they affect the whole week or, for that matter, the entire month. Does this person even know whether he or she is prepared to face the next day? In the system I am describing in this chapter, the goal is to keep looking at the bigger picture so you can be more thoughtful and effective in the use of your time.

Step 4: Use the Two-Page-to-One-Day System

Now you are ready to plan for the day. The two-page-to-one-day planning system that I use has five sections: a list of items to be done today (the action list), appointments and scheduled events, a section for phone calls, an expense and reimbursement section, and a full-page diary and work record.

When planning a single day, you are combining your master to-do list with your monthly calendar. First you enter all your appointments or scheduled activities from your monthly calendar. Then you move items from your master to-do list onto your action list for the day.

How many items you move depends on a few factors. The most obvious is how much of your time is already consumed by meetings, appointments, and other scheduled events. Don't plan to do too much if you do not have the time to do it. The idea is to end the day having completed all of your tasks and feeling good, not having to move tasks over to the next day. You do not want to create an action list that is impossible to complete and will leave you feeling unsuccessful at the end of the day. Be reasonable with yourself and realistic about what you can accomplish in any given day.

Another thing to consider is how many items on your master to-do list have to get done that day, those urgent and important items that have a deadline. (For more about urgency and importance, see the upcoming section about how to use a time management matrix.) Enter those tasks first. Next you can enter items that are important but not urgent. You will put them in as they fit into your daily schedule. Finally, you can list the general activities of life, which include shopping and picking up the dry cleaning. These things can and should be scheduled around the activities that are important to you.

You then prioritize all of your planned activities as they relate to the day. An A1 priority is something you have to get done today, A2 is the next priority, and so on.

You can use the extra sections of the diary page to record conversations, phone numbers, expenses, and other important information. This is a great place to make notes for yourself. The real goal is to bring your life together into one system that not only allows you to plan your life in accordance with your personal mission and goals but also allows you to retain important information for later use.

Step 5: Take Time for Planning and It Will Make Time for You

Believe it or not, effective time management requires a fair bit of a time commitment. Sometimes I hear complaints from people: "I do not have time to plan," or "Planning is too confining." However, as you get used to your system, you will become more efficient with it; in the end, you will find that you have more time in your life than you previously thought possible.

The most vital part of using this system is to spend an hour or so every week reflecting on your goals and commitments. Usually, I sit down on Sunday evening and work through my planner. (Monday night might work best for you as an actor.) I start with reviewing my master to-do list. I assess my previous accomplishments and generate a new priority list for the coming week. I eliminate things that are completed or are no longer important to me, and I add new items. These new items are usually handwritten items that came up throughout the week. I reprioritize my list and identify the things I wish to accomplish for the week, marking them as A priorities. I find that as I accomplish A priorities, the Bs tend to move up to be As. From that list, I move to the monthly calendar and review my scheduled appointments and routine events. I judge how busy I am for the week and visualize how my commitments can best work with my priorities and when I need to accomplish which items. In other words, I determine deadlines for certain items. I try to find scheduling opportunities where appointments and action items match up with things on my to-do list. Finally, I schedule the next day, Monday, as previously described.

Each night of the week, I sit down for ten minutes or so and schedule my next day's activities. I have found that by sitting down on Sunday, I often can keep much of my weekly goals and commitments in my head; I recall them more easily. However, when my life gets more complex and demanding, my weekly planner helps keep me on task and focused on the things I wish and need to do. In fact, the hardest time for me is when my life slows down and I do not use my planner as I should. These are the times when I have forgotten about work assignments and have missed meetings.

Try this planning system for thirty days, and I promise you will see a noticeable difference in your life. Instead of tying you down to a planner, this system will free you from things that are not important in your life. Time is one of your most valuable resources, and if you do not manage it, you are wasting it. As with any business organization, you must organize around your priorities—not only the ones that have immediate deadlines (e.g., putting out fires) but also the ones that are important to you and your career but lack deadlines (e.g., long-term planning). Over time, you will have fewer fires to deal with because you have already taken care of them. In addition, and I can attest to this myself, being in control of your life and knowing what needs to be done at any given time will help you sleep better at night.

As you get into the time management assignment, you may want to explore the various products and methods of planning available to you. You might consider using a PDA, or you might prefer a smaller calendar system than the one you began with. FranklinCovey (www.franklincovey.com) has some great products and a lot of information available online. You might also look into the Day-Timer (www.daytimer.com) and Day Runner (www.dayrunner.com) websites and their planning systems. These sites also provide expert advice, examples, and other helpful hints. Thirty days are all you need to start organizing your life, setting priorities, and accomplishing your goals. Take time to read through these sites. The information on them will help you better understand and use their products, which are all similar.

Using a Time Management Matrix

Another way to analyze and plan your activities is through the use of a *time management matrix*. Each and every activity we perform throughout the day can be categorized in one of four ways (Figure 3–2). Many people spend a good deal of their days performing activities found in quadrant IV (checking email and cell phone messages, watching TV, surfing the Internet) and in quadrant I (completing urgent, deadline-driven activities). Proper time management allows people to plan ahead—eliminating crises and

	URGENT	NOT URGENT
IMPORTANT	I Crises Pressing problems Deadline-driven projects	II Prevention Preparation Relationship building Recognizing new opportunities Planning Values clarification True recreation
NOT IMPORTANT	III Interruptions Many pressing matters Some phone calls Some mail Some reports Some meetings Many popular activities	IV Trivia, busy work Some mail Some phone calls Time wasters Pleasant activities Escape activities

Figure 3–2   Time Management Matrix (Source: Adapted from The Seven Habits of Highly Effective People, *Covey 1989, p. 151)*

deadline situations—and to stick to those important but not urgent activities of quadrant II. Time management allows you to control your time and focus on your priorities so you can get done the things you wish to complete, not allowing your time or energy to be directed by outside forces.

Many of us fall victim to the actions of other people and take on activities that have a sense of urgency but are not important, those activities found in quadrant III. Finding ways to deflect and politely decline these tasks frees you up to focus on your goals, not the goals of others. As each task comes your way, it is important to assess in which quadrant this new task falls and the proper action you need to take at this moment. Not all phone calls or emails need to be returned right away. A good tactic for these interruptions is to designate a block of time during each day to return phone calls and emails. This way you do not feel obligated to respond to everyone all the time.

As artists, it is sometimes difficult to say no or to turn down work of any kind. But sometimes no is the appropriate response when the work is not what you really want to do and will interfere with getting what you want. Successful time management allows you to identify your goals and priorities and provides the tools to stay focused to achieve those goals. Again, as Peter Drucker says, "Successful careers are not planned. They develop when people are prepared for opportunities because they know their strengths, their method of work, and their values" (Drucker 2005, p. 106).

Most people think that I am against spending any time in quadrant IV of the time management matrix. In fact, just the opposite is true. In our busy lives, we need time to do nothing, to goof off, if you will. As the saying goes, "All work and no play makes Jack a dull boy." But would it not be better and more enjoyable at the end of the day to play your favorite video game knowing that everything you set out to do that day was done and all that you needed to do tomorrow was already laid out for you. Now that is quadrant IV living!

Review, Evaluate, and Repeat

In Chapters 2 and 3, we have gone from the soup to the nuts of personal planning. We have gone from thinking about life accomplishments to organizing them in a day-to-day manner that turns goals into action. We have examined the external environment and looked for possible opportunities and threats. We have dug deep inside ourselves to acknowledge our own strengths and weaknesses. But things change, and you and your values will change with time. This is why evaluation and planning should be an ongoing activity. As new opportunities arise, you should adjust your thinking and planning to capitalize on opportunities.

The start of the year always represents a great time for reflection and action. But instead of making a New Year's resolution or two, how about redoing your goals in a way that lets you acknowledge your accomplishments, recognize goals not yet realized, and add new goals based on the present and future? In a way, this idea brings us back to doing a SWOT analysis and thinking about where you are now and where you want to go from there.

I encourage you to take the time to think through your plans for the next year as well as the years to come. You can and should do this any time you feel it is warranted. This type of thinking leads to strategic action and ultimately accomplishment. Companies call this strategic planning. But the value of it lies not in the creation of a formal document but in the process of really figuring out where you want to go next.

Notes from the Field: Opportunities in the Regional Theatre Market

Many opportunities for paid employment (besides acting) exist at the regional theatres across the country. The major League of Resident Theatre (LORT) companies and most theatres operating under other union contracts employ theatre artists in several capacities, either through administrative or educational positions. While websites often provide the most comprehensive and up-to-date information about a theatre's activities, you can use other resources to assist you in searching for a paid position in the arts, whether on a temporary or permanent basis.

The most useful of these is *Theatre Directory*, published annually by Theatre Communications Group (TCG), which has a wealth of information about over 440 theatres and organizations nationwide. This

continued

directory is organized alphabetically by theatre name and also by special interest, state, and budget—from 136 companies with a budget between $50,000 and $499,000 to 21 theatres with a budget that exceeds $10,000,000. And these are just the theatre companies that are members of TCG! Most communities have an organization that serves all its arts organizations and that, for example, may hold unified auditions on an annual basis and operate low-cost ticket booths in order to promote the local theatre companies (not just the professional theatres) and build a larger and more diverse audience.

Let's use Washington, DC, as an example. If you look at TCG's Theatre Directory, in the Theatre by States index, you'd think there were only ten theatre companies in DC. However, if you go to the Organizations and Associations section of the same publication, you'll find the listing for the League of Washington Theatres and its website: www.lowt.org. At this site, you'll discover that more than fifty nonprofit and for-profit professional theatres exist in the Washington area and that annual auditions are held in DC each June, attended by representatives of all the League's members. If you were looking at this site in January, you'd at least be able to scroll through each member's listing and put together a mailing. Each listing has a link to the theatre's website, so it's very easy to scan the season and see which shows remain, in addition to the information about where to send your materials to request an audition.

You probably have related interests that may qualify you for administrative or production work in one of these regional theatres. Most companies have busy education departments and require teaching artists to help with in-school and after-school programs, community-outreach initiatives, or study guides and teacher packets to accompany their season's plays. Some theatres have summer day camps for teens and need teachers in acting, movement, voice, and so on—and others have weekend and evening courses for local community members. These are all opportunities worth exploring for paid work, either to supplement your acting career or to begin a new path within your chosen field. Jobs at regional theatres often originate from paid internships. After a year as an intern, you would move into an assistant-level position in a particular department, such as public relations and marketing, development, production, general management, education, and artistic matters. Specific positions might include those working on press/publicity, graphics design and production, community programs, promotions, box office, grant writing, research, special events, board-related activities, stage management, company management, casting, and accounting. If you have the interest and the skills, full-time positions offer benefits such as vacation time and health care plans. You can weigh the options of taking full-time or part-time work and decide what you need. Not everyone has the temperament for a freelance actor lifestyle, but if you do, it may be possible for you to take acting jobs, in addition to having either a full-time or part-time job. If you have a full-time job, you may only be able to secure local acting jobs. If you take a part-time job, you will have greater flexibility to allow for travel when an out-of-town gig comes along. The time may come when your goals shift—if you decide to take a full-time theatre job, it doesn't mean the end to your acting career or your life's dream. It means you've made choices about what you need and what's important to you. Those priorities shift over the years, and to have a lifelong career in the theatre, you have to come to a sense of balance with those parts of the business over which you have control and those you don't. Many avenues exist, so don't feel you can choose only one road and have to stay on it for the rest of your life.

—C. W.

Action Items

- Determine each role you play in your life.
- Create your own personal mission statement.
- Research and review planning systems and methods for using them.
- Purchase a planning system (save the receipt).
- Create a master to-do list.
- Transfer important information and commitments to your planning system, including your monthly calendar.
- Follow the system for thirty days before making any adjustments as necessary.

■4■ Fiscal Management of Your Career

Four Financial Truths

While preparing for this book, I tried to use a variety of resources to express common and universal concepts, especially in regard to financial management. Financial management specialists—like people in other professions, our own included—have developed language that helps them better communicate with one another, but this sometimes leaves outsiders confused. One of the places where business jargon flows freely is *The Wall Street Journal*, but even there you can find simple and clear facts about personal financial management. Such is the case with an article by Jonathan Clements, "Amid Losses, 12 Financial Truths Persist" (Clements 2006a, p. 3). In this article, he discusses the uncertainty of the economy and the financial markets. People are always predicting that markets will go up or down, but no one knows for sure. The article's first four "truths" struck a core with me:

1. It's Hard to Cut Back
2. You'll Never Be Satisfied
3. Borrowings Have to Be Repaid
4. Fancy Cars and Expensive Clothes Aren't a Sign of Wealth

These four fairly straightforward ideas offer basic advice for anyone, but they seem particularly relevant for actors. Let's take a closer look at these four truths and see how they might relate to your life.

It's Hard to Cut Back

Depending on where you are in your life, you have probably experienced a certain level of life upgrading. This is when you pay more money for a better-quality product, for example, a nicer apartment with a washer and dryer included or with fewer roommates, a new car, or better clothes. But of course there was a price for all of this improvement. As you move along in life, these upgrades are good as long as you can continue to afford them. Unfortunately, if you're an actor whose income may fluctuate from year to year, it is hard to know whether you can afford these upgrades in the months or years to come. Be careful, and be patient—it will be hard to let go of things once you have them. It is easier never to have them in the first place.

You'll Never Be Satisfied

Over the years, there have been many studies on human happiness. Most come to a similar conclusion: No matter what our standard of living is, we will always strive for more. Once we have obtained a new standard of living, we get accustomed to that standard and naturally start to wish for more. This is known as hedonic adaptation, the cycle of moving from one accomplishment to the next. If we tell ourselves that we will be happy when we make more money or find a better place to live, once we have achieved these things, we will seek out and set goals for the next challenge. As an actor, you should know life and work is not about the product but the process, the journey to an end. Material objects and possessions are often not as satisfying as personal experiences and achievements.

Borrowings Have to Be Repaid

As anyone who has been in trouble with credit card debt will tell you, it is no fun paying off debt. Debt repayment usually takes a bit of sacrifice and is a long-term process, depending on the size of the debt. We live in a very debt driven society, but at some point in time someone—you or your family—will have to pay for your borrowing. Credit card companies and other lending institutions are quick to loan you money not because they want to help you but because they can make money off of you. The credit card industry generates over $30 billion per year in profits on their cards. It is a big business, and many of us need not be involved in it. In my thinking, this is how your money can work against you. Every month you pay a credit card bill, look at the amount of interest charged to you. Then think of what else you might have spent that money on rather than giving it to the credit card company.

Fancy Cars and Expensive Clothes Aren't a Sign of Wealth

The things we buy are not reflections of our wealth; rather, as Clements puts it, "they are a sign that somebody once had money but chose to borrow it. The money has since been spent, and the folks are poorer for it" (Clements 2006a, p. 3). Wealth is not what we wear or drive but a measure of what we have put away in the bank. However, when we see people with nice cars and fancy clothes, we might envy their lifestyle. Buying expensive things to try to look like we have the same status as someone else is sometimes called keeping up with the Joneses. But we need to be careful about our assumptions. Perhaps things are not as they seem. Wealth is not how much money we take home in our paycheck or the car we drive but how much money we have, our net worth, the sum of our savings minus our liabilities.

The simple truth is this: You must learn to live within your means. No matter what your income level, if you get in the habit of putting money aside and living within your means, you will be able to grow wealth. As your income level increases and you keep your spending in check, your savings potential will only increase. Money in the bank generates more money. Your money is working for you.

When people other than students have visited my Professional Aspects of Theater course, they almost always come up to me afterward to say that they wish they had taken a similar course when they were in college, or that they learned something new about managing money. In this industry, it seems that talking about money is taboo and that students are just expected to know what to do when they graduate from college. It seems to be a sink-or-swim mentality. This is a great shame. As is apparent by the number of people who file for bankruptcy each year and by the number of people who carry crippling debt, artists are not the only ones who have trouble managing their personal finances. However, the problem with talking about personal finances is that it is not very glamorous, nor are the results immediate. Financial management, like time management, requires discipline and persistence.

Notes from the Field:
Pain Is a Very Good Teacher

I had just moved to San Francisco from the East Coast and I'd been doing various temp jobs that didn't seem to make ends meet while developing material for a one-man show, so to supplement these activities I
began to build up a sizable amount of credit card debt. I ended up doing the revolving credit card thing where you keep transferring your
debt to a card with the lowest interest rate. By doing this I somehow
figured I was keeping the debt down. Of course, this meant turning a
blind eye to the total compounded amount, which was gradually grow-
ing month by month into a monster. Since the debt was spread over
several different cards and I never really put it all together in one lump
sum, it was easy to fool myself that everything was fine and dandy. At
this point, you get used to letting everything slide on by, figuring that it
is best not to worry and that you'll take care of it all *soon*. You'll take
care of it *next month*. Only next month never really happens because
next month arrives and, well, jeez, maybe it'll be the month *after* next
month. Gradually your little monthly payments grow from a pittance
into ransom for your firstborn child.

It was about this time that another writer/performer asked me to
direct a play. She had seen me doing my own material and thought I'd
be a good choice to direct her production. I was new in town and
looking to make a name for myself. It was an interesting challenge, and
I knew a lot about the subject matter, so I agreed to do it. Also, I was
very flattered because the person who offered this position was well
known in the underground theatre community, with great previous
press and reviews and somewhat of a following; plus, we agreed that
the idea of this play was so brilliant that it would be a sure-fire hit.

When I originally got involved in this person's project, I thought I
was just coming in as a director. I had no idea that somehow I would
end up actually producing the darn thing. I didn't know much about
directing and knew even less about producing. I was soon to learn a
great deal about both. Things began well enough when a benefit concert was thrown for our little production, which provided needed
seed money. I didn't know at the time, but that was actually the last
outside money we'd ever see for this production.

We auditioned the actors and booked a theatre. I'm not sure
why we did this. We didn't have any real money yet, just the start-up
money—a few hundred bucks. It was sort of like putting the cart

continued

before the horse. This is where things started to go very wrong. Like fools, we went ahead with preproduction, booking the theatre and gathering the actors and crew people. We were very naive, to say the least.

We did make somewhat of a plan. We got a local nonprofit to be our fiscal sponsor and thereby saved a little money on mailings and so on. We figured that we would apply for a grant and that since the theatre and one of the performers were well known, we'd be a shoo-in for the money. We thought we were so brilliant that we'd get it despite the fact that the subject of the play was not "community oriented" and did not have any "redeeming social value," which were two main requirements for this grant.

Needless to say, we didn't get this particular grant, so we tried for another one. The second grant from a local theatre foundation needed to be done through the theatre we were renting. The theatre became our sponsor. I spent days filling out all the paperwork, writing the proposals, and gathering the reviews and letters of support, only to find out that the theatre had submitted the paperwork incorrectly, thereby disqualifying our production. Upset about this, we canceled the booking and pulled out of this particular theatre.

The smart thing at this point would have been to wait to apply for other resources. The awful thing was, by this time we'd spent almost a year developing the project, and with the cast and crew already together, I guess I let my ego get the best of me by deciding we'd push ahead no matter what. After all, we live in a culture of instant gratification. It was very difficult to put the brakes on this production that we were all drooling to get done. There was no way I was going to spend all this time on a project and not have it come off. Plus, as I said, I was looking to make a name for myself. In order to do this, I figured I'd need to take some big risks.

So, we went to *another* theatre and booked it with my credit cards—cash advance. You know what happens with cash advance? They lend the money to you, all right, but at an interest rate of a bazillion percent. But I reasoned this little cash advance was only *temporary*. After all, it would soon be erased with our sure-fire hit, and I'd pay it off with money to spare. Heck, maybe I'd even wipe out my total debt. So I sunk the cash advance not only into the rental but also into the posters and postcards and whatever other promotional materials we needed to pull it off, as well as the cast, crew, and advertising, which included small quarter-page ads in local papers that were quite expensive. I was Mister Moneybags—and I didn't have a dime.

Then a strange thing happened that at first we thought of as a great boon. A documentary film opened about the *very same* subject matter as our play. It opened a couple of weeks before our play opened. How fantastic! What incredible timing! The gods were with us! People would go see the documentary and then check out our play! But that's not how it worked. People confused our posters with the posters for the film, even though they looked very different. The documentary was very well financed and promoted, and through a number of articles it put the subject matter in everyone's mind. The problem was that everything turned into grist for the documentary mill—no matter how we tried in our little feeble way to both join in and stand out as a separate entity, the documentary ended up with all the publicity, and we were like little cheerleaders in the background. In short, we were screwed. Many cynical theatre patrons thought we were doing our production as a last-second rush job in order to cash in on the popularity of the documentary, not realizing we'd been planning the thing for a year. Perhaps that was also the reason no one reviewed it.

Anyway, for whatever the actual reasons or maybe for no reason at all, the play took a dive. No one reviewed it. No one came to it. Many times the cast outnumbered the audience. Not only that, but the new theatre saw the "World Class Sucker" stamp on my forehead and asked if I wanted to book an extended run ahead of time. Now, I ask you, why on earth would you book an extended run for a production that hadn't even started yet? But we did. We did a six-week run for crickets—four shows a week. But I was honorable. Despite the fact that we made no money, I paid the cast and crew anyway.

In the aftermath of this disaster, the person whose play this was promised to have a benefit concert to bail me out, but that never materialized. How crazy is that? Who wants to have a benefit concert for a production that already happened? So yours truly was saddled with the additional debt. And the debt was for *someone else's* project! I just directed it! And since it wasn't even reviewed (despite hiring a publicist—for another wad of cash) and nobody saw it, it was as though the production never happened. I was *still* completely unknown in the theatre community.

I continued with my process of turning a blind eye to my rising debt and succeeded with this for another couple of years. Finally, though, all my chickens came home to roost one day when the debt

continued

became so great there was no way to dig out from under it. So I went into debt consolidation for a while, but after about a year of that, watching the debt not go down much but sort of hold steady, I finally declared personal bankruptcy. I made this decision because I still wanted to move onward, and I needed some sort of money to promote myself as a writer and performer. I'd somehow managed to enslave myself to the system, and I hadn't even begun to do my own work. I'd thrown it all away on someone else. How was I going to have any money to do anything when 75 percent of my income was going toward rent and the debt?

After that mess, I began to do my own theatre projects, consisting of eccentric one-man shows and plays that I'd written. I have since become known locally and have even racked up a few awards, and in the strange way these things happen, other people soon began to produce my work. This was good because I'd lost all my money on my foolish adventures. It has been several years now, and oddly enough the credit card companies hound me weekly for new cards. Just a couple of weeks ago in *one day alone* I got solicited by seven different card companies! I don't take the bait. I've had a steady day job the past few years that pays the bills, and I've avoided piling up new debt like the plague. I sort of wish someone had asked me to write about my creative process instead of my idiotic financial history. But perhaps this will somehow be a cautionary tale. As Stanley Kubrick once said, "Pain is a very good teacher."

—A. C.

Your Money or Your Life

In Joe Dominguez and Vicki Robin's book *Your Money or Your Life: Transforming Your Relationship with Money and Achieving Financial Independence* (1992), they discuss a concept they call *life energy*. They define our life energy as "our allotment of time here on earth, the hours of precious life available to us. When we go to our jobs we are trading life energy for money" (Dominguez and Robin 1992, p. 54). Time is money; we have all heard that expression before. But how we spend our time is a decision we make each and every day. If we spend most of our time in the pursuit of money, what is left for the rest of our life? Conversely, the things that we spend our money on demand that we spend time making money to purchase those things. For example, we all need a place to live and food to eat. In order to pay for these things, we need to work and earn money. The more expensive the rent and food, the more we have to earn, which could translate into the need to work more hours or to receive higher pay per hour worked. Understanding how you spend your money is the first step in financial planning.

A company spends a great deal of time understanding the flow of money in and out of the organization and managing its investments. Bookkeepers record payables and receivables, and accountants create income statements and balance sheet reports. How much time do you spend analyzing your financial position?

Recording Your Spending Habits

Your first assignment in this chapter is to record how you spend your money in a given month. In a way, you are creating a personal cash flow statement. You will record how much money you take in, how much money you spend, and what is left at the end of the month—your savings. This exercise will give you a clear picture of where your money is going and how you might make meaningful adjustments in your earning and spending habits.

Warning: Money seems to carry an emotional attachment to it. This exercise is not about right or wrong, and there is no winning or losing—think Viola Spolin—because there is no right or wrong way to spend money. It is about taking an objective look at how your organization spends its resources (time and money). Please refrain from adjusting your spending during this task; otherwise, you will only skew the results. You will make observations about your spending after you complete the assignment. Only then will you have a complete picture of your monthly expenses.

Starting on the first day of the month, begin tracking every penny of your spending. This includes everything from your morning cup of coffee to your evening cocktail. Your record should include those things you paid for with cash and those you charged on credit. The easiest way to do this is to ask for receipts on items purchased (which is generally a good habit to start for tax purposes) or to write notes in your planner.

As you begin to collect receipts, you can start to create categories for these items. Category examples include groceries, dining out, clothing, entertainment and leisure, transportation, job expenses, and banking (if your bank charges you monthly service fees or ATM charges, those are expenses). Keep an eye out for life's little hidden expenses: newspapers, vending machines, quick snacks. You can decide how to best catalog your spending areas once you have collected enough receipts. You will also need to include monthly bills such as rent, phone, utilities, and loan payments (Figure 4–1).

Finally, you will record how you receive money. This includes money from work, support from parents, and earnings from odd jobs.

When you are done, you should have an exact account of all the money that came in during the month and all the money you spent. Revenues minus expenses equals net income; this is the equation of an income statement. At the bottom of that equation will be the money you have left over or the amount you overspent for the period (Figure 4–2). Remember to remain calm and objective.

Let's work with the hypothetical numbers shown in our sample statement and see how you might be able to make some positive adjustments. First, let us look at what we will call fixed

Category	Monthly Expense
Rent	$975
Car Payment	150
Car Insurance	75
Credit Card Interest	50
ATM Fees	16
Phone—Land Line	35
Cell Phone	84
Student Loan	250
Credit Card	100
Cable/Internet	95
Electricity/Utilities	85
Gym Membership	100
Food	150
Misc.	150
Total Expenses	**$2,315**

Figure 4–1 Personal Monthly Expense Statement

Revenues/Earnings	
Full-Time Job	$1,700
Odd Jobs	800
Total Earnings	**$2,500**
Net Income	**$185**

Figure 4–2   Personal Monthly Earnings Statement

expenses. These expenses usually come in the form of a monthly bill and might include your rent, utilities, phone, insurance, cable bill, Internet service, and/or gym membership fees. You should examine each one of these expenses and ask yourself several questions. Do you use this service to the fullest extent? Are there cheaper alternatives? What is the minimum level of service you can accept? Are you paying too much for the services you use? Let's demonstrate with a couple of examples.

Let's say you live in New York City and have a membership to an area fitness center. You use this gym to take aerobic classes and work out in the weight room. But the membership fee is a bit pricey, and you are not always as loyal to your workout routine as you would like, although your new time management system is improving that. A few blocks down the street is the local YMCA, which offers a similar setup without all of the amenities. Since the fee is $20 cheaper each month ($240 per year) for the YMCA membership and you do not really use the extra amenities of your current gym, you decide to go ahead and change your membership when your current one expires.

However, if you routinely spend a great deal of time at the gym and do use most of the amenities your current fitness center offers, changing memberships only for the savings will leave you disappointed. Therefore, it would probably not be wise to switch just to save $20 per month. You truly have to decide for yourself the value, both financial and personal, of the things you pay for. Only you can decide whether you are willing to give up certain things to save a few dollars.

You also need to compare the costs and benefits of your gym membership against other activities that require money; for example, by paying for the gym, you may have less money available for going out with your friends. If you are living on a tight budget, you should potentially give up a few things until you are better situated financially.

Now let's turn to your cable television bill. You might ask yourself how often you watch television. What do you watch? Is it worth the money and time you give to it? Are there alternatives? If you do not watch a great deal of television, you might consider canceling your cable service altogether. Perhaps you want to cancel the premium channels and go down to the basic service. You might decide that instead of watching movies on cable you would rather use the money to rent current movies. The decision is yours.

Although we might be talking about only a few dollars here and there, those dollars will add up. If you reduce your fixed expenses by, say, just $50 a month, by the end of the year you will have saved $600. That's a pretty good start.

Now our attention must go to the wild and wonderful world of your *variable expenses*. Apart from fixed expenses, these are the other things you spend your money on: coffee, newspapers, drinks with friends, dinners out, music CDs, DVDs, and all the other things that make up your daily life. Divide this list into two subcategories: essential and nonessential. Essential expenses include food, transportation, and clothing. Nonessentials include entertainment, take-out food, and other random purchases.

You should work with the essential variable expenses in much the same manner as you did with your fixed expenses. Are there cheaper alternatives for these things? If so, is buying the less expensive items acceptable to you and your values? For example, eating fresh, natural foods could be very important to you, so buying lower-quality produce may be unacceptable. And that's okay. Work with what you can accept, and try to bring your expenses down as best you can. If you feel that certain changes require great sacrifice, you probably won't stick with them. If you feel the changes are acceptable, you probably will be able to live with them over the long term. You are changing habits, and that will take time.

Next, move on to your nonessential expenses. This part of the process will be a bit more emotional, and it will also provide you with the greatest opportunity to save money. As human beings, we fall into patterns and habits. Probably the predictable habits for most people are their morning routines, the ones they follow from the time they wake up, shower, eat, and drink their coffee to the time they arrive at work. In David Bach's book *The Automatic Millionaire* (2003), he describes what he calls the Latte Factor. During one of his lectures, he asked a participant to describe her morning routine and what she did. It turns out that each morning this person purchased a muffin and a latte from a local coffee shop. The cost to her was $5 per day. She worked five days a week; therefore, her breakfast was costing her $25 per week. In a month, she spent $100. In a year, she spent approximately $1,200 on muffins and latte! This is the Latte Factor. Now let's find out what yours is.

When evaluating your monthly variable expenses, try to find the areas in which you might save money. By making simple adjustments to daily routines, you can make a substantial difference in your financial well-being by saving $5 here, $25 there—add up the changes you can make and multiply the sum by a year, and you will be looking at a good deal of money. You should also look at the services you are getting from companies such as banks. Are you being charged for your checking account? If you take money out of an ATM that is not your bank's machine, do you get charged for that? Could you switch to a better phone plan to reduce your monthly bill? Dig deep and see where you might save a few dollars here and there. It can really pay off.

Once you have made spending adjustments, your new cash flow statement might look like the one shown in Figure 4–3.

In this example, we have managed, in a few easy steps, to reduce monthly expenses by $115.

Congratulations, you just created your very own budget. Your personal cash flow statement can serve as a tool for your financial planning, not only in the short term but also in the long term.

Continuing further, you might cost out all of your expenses for an entire year simply by multiplying your monthly expenses by twelve months (Figure 4–4). This would allow you to determine your earning needs for a given year. This longer view will help you see the real power in making just a few simple financial adjustments. It will also help you determine your earning needs for a twelve-month period, in other words, how much money you will need to live for a year (Figure 4–5).

In this example, we managed to reduce the annual expenses by $1,380. That is a pretty good raise. Understanding how you

Category	Original Monthly Expense	Adjusted Monthly Expense
Rent	$975	$975
Car Payment	150	150
Car Insurance	75	75
Credit Card Interest	50	50
ATM Fees	16	0
Phone—Land Line	35	0
Cell Phone	84	80
Student Loan	250	250
Credit Card	100	100
Cable/Internet	95	55
Electricity/Utilities	85	85
Gym Membership	100	80
Food	150	150
Misc.	150	150
Total Expenses	**$2,315**	**$2,200**

Figure 4–3   Adjusted Monthly Expense Statement

Category	Monthly Expense	Yearly Expense
Rent	$975	$11,700
Car Payment	150	1,800
Car Insurance	75	900
Credit Card Interest	50	600
ATM Fees	0	0
Phone—Land Line	0	0
Cell Phone	80	960
Student Loan	250	3,000
Credit Card	100	1,200
Cable/Internet	55	660
Electricity/Utilities	85	1,020
Gym Membership	80	960
Food	150	1,800
Misc.	150	1,800
Total Expenses	**$2,200**	**$26,400**

Figure 4–4   Annual Expenses

Revenues/Earnings		
	Monthly Income	Yearly Income
Full-Time Job	$1,700	$20,400
Odd Jobs	800	9,600
Total Earnings	**$2,500**	**$30,000**
Net Income	**$300**	**$3,600**

Figure 4–5   Annual Income

spend your money and control needless spending is just the first step in financial management. The goal of financial planning is not just to make enough money but also to start saving and ultimately investing that money—in other words, the goal is to have your money work for you.

Determining Your Net Worth

Setting financial goals is an important step in gaining financial stability. In addition to understanding your spending habits, you also need to understand your net worth. Your financial net worth is the sum of your assets minus any financial obligations or liabilities, that is, the things you own minus the things you owe. In corporate speak, the report that shows these numbers is called a *balance sheet*. A balance sheet is a snapshot of an organization's financial position at any given moment. The value of determining your net worth is to identify areas that need to be addressed and to set achievable goals, just like understanding your spending habits.

Assets for a business include available cash, savings, property, and equipment. This is similar to the assets individuals have. To determine your assets, begin by listing all of your cash, bank accounts, and investments. You may also have noncash assets, for example, a car, a home, and such valuables as musical instruments. Assets are those things that have a dollar value and can easily be transferred into cash. During this exercise, you do not want to give value to everything you own, just the things that have significant value or are typically traded or resold. Could you sell a particular item on eBay? If so, how much do you think you could reasonably get for it? Check and see for yourself; perhaps what you thought had value is being given away online. After your evaluation, you might generate a list of assets like the one shown in Figure 4–6.

Next, move on to your financial obligations or loans. These are called *liabilities*. Liabilities include anything that you owe beyond thirty days. For example, they do not include monthly phone or water bills or your rent, but they do include credit card balances if those balances are not paid off each month. Your liabilities might look something like the list shown in Figure 4–7.

In our example, this person's net worth is –$22,046. For someone who just graduated from college, this financial snapshot may not be such a bad thing. After all, many of us obtained higher education through the use of student loans, which proved to be a valuable investment. For someone in their fifties, however, this snapshot may spell serious trouble.

Assets	Total
Cash	$100
Checking Account	1,500
Savings	5,524
Car	2,500
Total Assets	**$9,624**

Figure 4–6 Personal Assets Statement

Liabilities	Total
Credit Card	$3,500
Student Loan	25,670
Car	2,500
Total Liabilities	**$31,670**
Net Worth	**–$22,046**

Figure 4–7 Personal Liabilities Statement

As with the previous exercise, the purpose of understanding your financial position by determining your net worth is not to pass judgment or to make you feel bad. The point is to shed light on your financial situation and allow you to change for the better. This type of analysis allows you to be proactive with your money and to make the right decisions for your long-term success. I am not trying to turn you into a certified public accountant, but as an artistic entrepreneur you must have a basic understanding of your financial well-being as well as recognize when you need professional assistance. In Chapter 5, I will discuss some of the golden rules of money management and how they can help you and your business achieve financial and personal success.

Let us end where we began, and as we move through the following chapters of this book, let us keep in mind the wisdom of Jonathan Clements and his four financial truths (Clements 2006a, p. 3):

1. It's Hard to Cut Back
2. You'll Never Be Satisfied
3. Borrowings Have to Be Repaid
4. Fancy Cars and Expensive Clothes Aren't a Sign of Wealth

Wealth is not a measure of what we buy or the things we have. Wealth is a measure of the financial resources we have available to us. It is our net worth; it is our money in the bank.

Action Items

- Track your cash flow (money in and money out) for one month. Be sure to account for ATM fees, bank charges, credit card interest, and so on.
- From your cash flow statement, create a monthly budget and a yearly budget.
- Create your personal balance sheet to determine your net worth.
- Continue working with your daily planner system.

Fiscal Planning and Goal Setting

In the previous chapter, you learned two things. First, you learned that you *do* have *extra* money, the savings you can get after examining your spending habits carefully in relationship to your needs rather than just spending money on what you want. I hate to use the word *budget*, but that is exactly what you created. By examining your spending patterns, you created a *budget* for your monthly expenses. Second, you learned your *net worth*, the money you would have left over if you paid all your debt today. Even if you discovered that you have a negative net worth, as you will soon learn, there are many ways to change that negative into a positive. Your net worth is the bottom line to all your financial matters. Empowered by these discoveries, you can begin to plan for your future and start to set and meet your financial goals.

In business terms, budget and net worth documents would be called *budgeted income statements* and *balance sheets*, respectively. By combining these with *cash flow statements*—documentation of cash receipts and expenditures—organizations can gain a more accurate picture of their financial standing as well as determine how best to use their money. Through the use of these statements, you too can better control and manage your money. Best of all, you can begin to have your money work for you instead of the other way around.

Pay Yourself First

Paying yourself first is the first tried and true rule of financial planning; you must pay yourself first before you pay anything or anyone else. In this way you put your own personal financial goals ahead of any other priorities. Doing so ensures that with each paycheck, you are putting money aside to accomplish your personal financial goals.

Paying yourself first, especially when you are starting your career, does not have to be a great sacrifice. I would recommend against it being so, as you will be less likely to stick with your plan if it becomes a burden. Instead, choose a sum of money that, given your personal spending habits, is reasonable for you to put away as savings. While it does not need to be a huge amount, it should be a consistent amount, that is, you should put the same amount of money aside each time you get paid. For example, if you get paid on a regular schedule, you could save $25 each week or each paycheck, depending on when you get paid. If you get paid on an irregular basis, you could put aside 5 percent or 10 percent of each paycheck. Hopefully, this way it will become *automatic* or second nature for you to do this every time you generate income.

In today's technology-driven society, it is also possible for you to make these payments to yourself electronically (the overriding theme of David Bach's *The Automatic Millionaire* [2003]). Through direct deposit, you can open a special account separate from your main checking/debit card account and have some of your money automatically deposited into that account. Or you can create a monthly direct transfer from your checking account to a savings account. These types of arrangements make saving seamless and regular—you don't have to think about it once you set up your system. This removes not only the burden of saving but also the temptation of changing your mind. A simple savings account should suffice for now. In case of an extreme emergency, you should be able to get at your money easily but not too easily.

My First Financial Advisor: My Mother

I cannot write this section without giving credit to my mother, my first financial advisor. My mother always told me to pay myself first, to put money aside to spend later for emergencies or a home, or just to have it earning interest. My father credits my mother for her determination to always save a little bit of money for the future, even when they thought they did not have any to spare. But, alas, young men often do not listen to their mothers and therefore pay the bitter consequences. If I had saved just $25 a week, or $1,300 a year, I, twenty years later, would have saved a total of $26,000. Moreover, with the addition of compound interest at a 7 percent yearly interest rate, I would have $57,025 saved for the future. Adding another twenty years, $25 a week, and 7 percent interest, I would have a total savings of $277,692. As you can see, it is not so much about the amount of money you add to your savings account as when you start to do it. It is all about the power of compound interest.

Notes from the Field: A Note on Saving

A good strategy for increasing your wealth is to pay yourself first; that is, invest in your future by saving for yourself before you take on other financial obligations. This is not to suggest that you should delay paying your debts as you agreed to do when you originally borrowed money. Instead, before buying new accessories or taking on more debt, make sure that you have some money going into an account for your long-term needs. Setting up a retirement account is the best place to start because of the tax advantages it provides. Use the money that you have left after paying yourself to pay your debts or to improve your current lifestyle.

You pay a high cost when you wait to save money. Do not wait to start saving until you can afford to—you will have to save much more when you try to catch up and make up for lost time. The decade between ages 22 and 32 is a key savings period. By missing this one decade it can take another three decades to catch up because of the effect of compound interest on your savings. With investing, time is on your side. Use time to your advantage, and start saving as soon as you start working. A basic tenet of how compound interest works is this: The longer you have to invest, *even with small amounts of money*, the greater your future wealth and financial security. Don't wait.

—R. F.

The Power of Compound Interest

When people think about saving money, they often forget about compound interest. If you save $1,300 the first year at 7 percent interest, the interest adds $91 to your account, for a total of $1,391. The following year, if you add another $1,300, you'll earn interest of $188.37, or $2,691 times 7 percent. As you can see from Figure 5–1, the power of compound interest over time has an incredible boosting power to your savings. Not only is the steady investment of money working for you, but the interest you receive is also adding to the total for which interest is being calculated.

Establishing Financial Goals

Once you are paying yourself first, you need to establish goals for your money. These goals will include short- and long-term financial strategies and can be broken down into the following categories:

1. Paying off and managing bad debt
2. Establishing a cash reserve fund
3. Short-term savings
4. Long-term and retirement savings

We'll examine each of these goal categories in this chapter.

Number of Years	Without Interest	With Compound Interest
1	$1,300	$1,391
2	2,600	2,879
3	3,900	4,472
4	5,200	6,176
5	6,500	7,999
10	13,000	19,218

Figure 5–1   Compound Interest Table

Paying Off and Managing Bad Debt

In a country awash with debt, it may not seem like a big deal to have a bit of debt. But as you know from the previous chapter, eventually you will have to pay off your debt. In the meantime, lenders are making money off of the interest they charge against their loans. It is big business for these companies, but you do not have to be one of their customers.

Not all debt is created equal. There is good debt and there is bad debt. Deciding whether debt is good or bad usually depends on two factors: the amount of interest being charged and the purpose of the debt. Good debt is typically used to buy such things as cars, homes, and education. A small amount of credit card debt can also be good since it provides a record of your ability to manage and repay debt. However, a large amount of credit card debt can be a very bad thing. Other high-interest loans can also damage your financial health. You are having debt trouble if you find yourself unable to keep up with monthly payments or, in the case of credit card debt, you are making only the minimum payments.

Let's revisit an example from Chapter 4. Figures 5–2 and 5–3 show the balance sheet previously presented in Figures 4–6 and 4–7, respectively, but this time we have recorded the interest rates we are either receiving or paying.

In this example, the student loan meets the criteria for good debt: fairly low interest rates for good things, things we need to succeed. The credit card debt, on the other hand, would be con-

Assets	Total	Interest Rate
Cash	$100	—
Checking Account	1,500	0%
Savings	5,524	2%
Car	2,500	—
Total Assets:	**$9,624**	

Figure 5–2 Personal Assets with Interest

Liabilities	Total	Interest Rate
Credit Card	$3,500	18%
Student Loan	25,670	4.5%
Car	2,500	7%
Total Liabilities	**$31,670**	
Net Worth	**–$22,046**	

Figure 5–3   Personal Liabilities with Interest

sidered bad debt. Even if you paid $100 a month on that credit card, it would take you fifty months to pay it off! In other words, in fifty months you will have spent $5,000 paying off a $3,500 loan! That is not a very wise way to use your money.

Here is another way to look at it. In this particular scenario, this individual has enough money in savings to pay off the credit card debt in full. That money is earning 2 percent interest, or $70 a year. However, this person is being charged 18 percent, or $630 a year, for borrowing the same amount of money. This person is losing nearly $560 a year on interest by not paying off the credit card bill. When you are paying out more in interest than you are taking in, you are losing money. Your money is not working for you, it is working against you—not a wise business decision or a good use of your money. Unless there is a particular need for this money in the near future, this person would be wise to pay off the credit card. Let's face it, in today's world everyone accepts credit cards; if this person got into a real pinch after using savings to pay off that debt, he or she could use credit again to get by and then pay it off later. In the meantime, he or she would save a bit of money by eliminating the interest being charged. Paying off the bad debt should be this person's priority.

Once the person has paid off the credit card debt—in this case, with a single payment—the new balance sheet looks like Figure 5–4.

Now all that remains is good debt. The person could try to find options to reduce the interest on these loans, but it is not a pressing matter. Note that this person's net worth remained unchanged. Using an asset to pay off a liability leaves a zero change

Assets	Total	Interest Rate
Cash	$100	—
Checking Account	1,500	0%
Savings	2,024	2%
Car	2,500	—
Total Assets	**$6,124**	

Liabilities	Total	Interest Rate
Student Loan	25,670	4.5%
Car	2,500	7%
Total Liabilities	**$28,170**	
Net Worth	**–$22,046**	

Figure 5–4   Adjusted Net Worth

in net worth. But since that debt has been removed, added assets (savings) will begin to positively affect net worth. This person might consider increasing monthly savings by the amount of the average credit card payment he or she had been making.

Credit Card Usage
Not all credit card debt needs to be bad debt. If you use a credit card to cover temporary cash shortfalls on important purchases *and* you pay off the balance in the following month or within a few months, you are using your credit card wisely. As you saw in the previous example, maintaining a credit card balance can be costly. If you are paying only your minimum monthly payment and watching your balance increase each month, you have a problem that needs to be addressed. Paying off bad debt should be the first priority when beginning your financial planning process.

Playing the Interest Game
Another way to improve your financial situation is to play the interest game. You should try to obtain the best possible interest rate you can. For savings accounts, it should be as high as possible; for debts, it should be the reverse, as low as possible. Once you begin to make changes in your financial picture, you may im-

prove your credit rating and therefore qualify for lower interest rates on debts.

If you are dealing with high credit card debt, you may consider moving it to another company to take advantage of lower introductory interest rates. Your first priority is to pay off your credit card balance in full, but changing companies may help in the short term. Be careful to read the fine print on these offers, as it may turn out that once an introductory rate expires, you were better off with the card you originally had.

Consolidation loans may also prove helpful in reducing your interest rate on loans. However, consolidation loans should be used not as a vehicle for borrowing more money but as a way to save money. You need to be committed to and focused on paying off your debt. For people without the necessary financial discipline, taking out consolidation loans or accepting introductory rate offers can lead to even more debt. You need to be careful.

Establishing a Cash Reserve Fund

Most people get into trouble with bad debt because they did not have cash when they needed it most, used credit cards to get through the rough times, and then are unable (or unwilling) to pay off the borrowed money. Actors are typically some of the most financially responsible people I know, but once you get into financial trouble, it is sometimes hard to get out. And though I am not an actor, I have been in the nonprofit theatre business most of my career, and I know how hard it can be to make ends meet. In 2004, the average American household carried a credit card debt of $9,312 with an average interest rate on that debt of 11.84 percent (Kelley 2005). In 2005, the U.S. savings rate was negative for the first time since 1933 (Clements 2006b). One way to avoid the accumulation of bad debt is to have cash on hand to pay for life's unexpected expenses. This way, when you need extra money to pay for new headshots or to move into a new apartment, you are borrowing the money from your best lender—yourself.

The rule of thumb when it comes to establishing a reserve fund is to have enough money to cover three to six months of your monthly expenses. The more erratic your earnings, the more you need to put away. Actors should set a goal of saving as much as six months of their living expenses since their earnings tend to be irregular. Since you established your monthly spending habits by completing the exercise in the previous chapter, you know exactly how much you need to save: Multiplying your monthly cost of living by six will give you your next financial goal.

What This Money Is For
Although it will take a bit of doing to save six months' worth of living expenses, once you have your cash reserve in place, you will be very glad you made the effort. In the beginning, as you are establishing your cash reserve, you can use the money saved for life's little financial surprises or for those things you may need to advance your career. However, you need to be very guarded about what you use this money for, not to the extent that you take on bad debt, but so that you use your savings wisely to advance your career and financial goals—building up this savings account being one of them.

Once you have established a six-month reserve by paying yourself first and eliminating bad debt, sit back and enjoy the financial freedom. Think about this for a minute. A lot the strain of being an actor is getting the next paycheck or paying gig. Actors tend to be on the financial edge all the time and must work to keep from going under. Having money in the bank allows for artistic freedom. When you and your career are ready, this fund will allow you to take the time to audition and to land your next acting job rather than going back to work at an office or restaurant. This money will allow you to move freely from one job to the next without the anxiety of working a side job.

Establishing a reserve fund will prepare you for life's unexpected costs as well as provide you with the freedom to make calm and rational career moves without the immediate worry of money.

Where to Put Your Reserve Fund
Your cash reserve fund needs to be liquid. In other words, you need to be able to get your money quickly without penalty or loss of earned interest. When an emergency strikes, you want your money to be at the ready. Three types of savings options are suitable: a typical savings account, a money market savings account, and a certifi-

cate of deposit (CD). The trick is to try to get the best possible interest on your money while still keeping it liquid—which is not always easy. With a six-month reserve fund, you should keep the bulk of it in a traditional savings account and a smaller percentage in a three- to six-month CD. This way in the worst-case scenario, say, if you were unemployed for all six months, you would first use up the money in your savings account, during which time your CD would come due and you could withdraw that amount without penalty for early withdrawal.

Certificate of Deposit versus Money Market Account

A CD requires you to invest money for a certain length of time and guarantees a fixed rate of return (interest) for that entire time. CDs usually require a minimum deposit, typically starting at about $1,000. Money invested in a CD is less liquid than money placed in a savings account. You are not free to take your money out whenever you want. With CDs, you must invest your money for a specific time: from three months to up to five years. The longer you commit your money, the higher the interest rate. You can withdraw your money prior to its maturity date, but you will be required to pay a penalty.

Money market accounts are a kind of savings account in which you have to deposit at least the required amount. For this reason, a money market account usually pays a higher interest rate than a regular savings account does, although the interest rate varies day to day depending on the performance of the financial markets. Unlike a CD, you may withdraw money from a money market account at any time. In fact, most money market accounts come with checkbooks. With some accounts, you may be required to keep a minimum balance.

Short-Term Savings

Short-term financial goals have a two- to five-year time frame. These goals might focus on buying a car or a home. Of course, if you're currently living in a large metropolitan area where you don't need a car and houses are very expensive, these short-term goals may seem unrealistic, and perhaps you are right. However, another good financial rule is to not borrow money to buy depreciating assets. In other words, for purchases like computers, cell phones, furniture, and other high-priced items, it is better to save up and buy them out right rather than buying them with credit. If you borrow money for these items, they are more expensive because you have to pay the interest on the loan all the while they are depreciating in value.

In order to gauge what your short-term financial goals should be, you need to check in with the personal mission statement you created in Chapter 3. Where do you see yourself in five years? What would you like to accomplish? Travel? Purchase an apartment or home? Buy a car? These are goals for your short-term financial savings, and each will translate into a dollar goal: $5,000 for an overseas vacation, 20 percent down on a mortgage, $5,000 for a car. Now you have real numbers to work with.

Because these goals are further in the future and because you have already created your reserve fund, you can put your savings for these goals into investments that require a longer period of time in order to gain a higher interest rate, thus making your money work for you. Investment options for this category may include long-term CDs, money market mutual funds, and treasury bonds.

Simply put, with short-term financial goals, you are saving up for big-ticket items that you may want in the future. Once you have saved all the money, or at least a good portion of what you'll pay, you can go out and get these items. By saving the money first, you are not only earning interest but also avoiding interest payments on the loan you would have otherwise taken. Saving for these goals also develops the financial discipline that will benefit you throughout your lifetime. Who knows—in five years maybe you'll change your mind and just keep your money in the bank.

Money Market Mutual Funds and Treasury Bonds

Money market mutual funds are accounts that combine the money of many investors to buy several kinds of investments, including stocks, bonds, real estate, and so on. There is risk because with mutual funds no one insures your investment. If the price of the fund drops, you lose money. Mutual funds are safer than individual stocks because collectively buying lots of different stocks and bonds through a mutual fund lowers your individual risk. This is known as *diversification*. Mutual funds are professionally managed by financial experts and charge a management fee to investors. With mutual funds, you have the freedom to withdraw your money at any time. However, at the time you sell your shares (the number of units you own in the fund), you are paid what the shares are worth *that day*. Their worth may be higher or lower than what you paid for them.

When you buy U.S. treasury bonds, you are basically lending money to the federal government. There are two kinds of U.S. bonds.

1. EE bonds are also called discount bonds. When you buy these bonds, you pay half their face value, or half the value printed on the bond. For example, you pay $50 for a $100 bond. Each year that you keep the bond, its value increases as interest adds up. Even after the bond reaches the value stamped on it, the bond will continue to earn interest. Bonds earn interest for 30 years from the date they were issued. This may be important to you if you were given bonds as a child—they may have stopped working for you by now. Check into their date of purchase to determine whether they are still earning interest.
2. I bonds are sold at their face value ($50 for a $50 bond). They earn interest and can be cashed in to pay for college. They are tax free meaning you do not pay taxes on the interest you earn from these bonds. The interest rate on these bonds is adjusted every six months. However, the reduction in taxes might outweigh a low interest rate.

The money you invest in bonds is backed by the full faith and credit of the federal government. Unfortunately, buying U.S. bonds ties up your money for five years. After that time, you can redeem your bonds without penalty. Interest rates on U.S. bonds are generally low because this type of investment has lower risks.

Long-Term and Retirement Savings

Long-term savings goals go well beyond the five years of short-term goals and should include creating a retirement account. Your long-term savings goals may also include saving for a child's college education. When people think of retirement accounts, they often immediately think of Individual Retirement Accounts (IRAs). However, many people do not understand how these accounts work and why they are so valuable to one's overall financial plan.

How Classic IRAs Work

The purpose of an IRA is to provide individuals with financial savings to assist them during their retirement years. You can begin investing in an IRA at any time; however, you cannot begin to withdraw funds until you are age $59\frac{1}{2}$. You can invest your money in an IRA tax free, up to the allowable limits of the law. These limits are set by the U.S. government and change periodically. You pay taxes on your contributions and earnings when you begin to withdraw the money. While you are saving and earning interest for your retirement, you are also saving money on your personal taxes. However, there is a penalty if you withdraw your money prior to age $59\frac{1}{2}$. In addition, you usually must begin to take money out of your account by age $70\frac{1}{2}$.

You can set up an IRA with your local bank or financial service provider. Each plan offers you a choice of how to invest your money, using traditional terms such as aggressive, conservative, or moderate. Traditional investment strategy suggests that as you near retirement age, you want to move your money into more conservative investments that bear less risk due to the ups and downs of the economy, although some financial advisors are beginning to challenge that wisdom. You and your financial advisor can determine where you feel most comfortable on this scale. In general, as you get older you also want to move your money into investment accounts that are more liquid.

Think of it this way: Your IRA is your reserve fund for the last twenty to thirty years of your life. You are going to need a lot of money, and it is best to start saving now. Again, you do not need to save a lot of money from each paycheck, but you should save something.

401(k) Plans and IRAs

If you have regular employment, you may be eligible for your company's 401(k) plan, or a 403(b) or 457 plan if you work for a nonprofit company or the government, respectively. A 401(k) retirement plan works like a classic IRA but is coordinated by an employer. This is a great way to get started even if you do not see yourself staying at a company for too long. You need to take advantage of this while you can. Typically, employers automatically deduct your retirement contributions from your paycheck. These pretax deductions reduce your taxable income. Employers may even contribute money up to a certain percentage of your total salary. An employer 401(k) plan is an opportunity you should not pass up.

IRAs and 401(k)s are excellent investments for retirement that you need to start now. Remember the value of compound interest? Now add the pretax or tax-deductible savings, deferred tax growth on your savings, and possible employer contributions! Retirement plans offer benefits you should not refuse. Again, as with your cash reserve fund, you can have contributions to your IRA automatically deducted from your checking account on a regular basis.

Once you have reached this level of savings complexity, the best advice I can give is to see a financial planner. You can seek help from the investment department of a bank you like or from such companies as Merrill Lynch, ING, or A.G. Edwards & Sons, to name a few. Ask your friends who helps them with financial planning. Call some recommended firms and ask to meet with someone.

If you are self-employed and/or run a small business, you might be able to take advantage of two other retirement accounts: SEP IRA (Simplified Employee Pension plan) and One-Person 401(k)/Profit Sharing Plan. For individuals who qualify, these plans offer some exceptional benefits; you can discuss them with your advisor.

How Much Money Should I Save?

I understand that it may seem nearly impossible to consider paying yourself first and putting away money for a reserve fund and retirement account. But you need to begin sometime, so why not now? Again, the amount you save does not have to be a great sacrifice to you and your lifestyle, but it should be something.

From the work you did in Chapter 4, you know you can adjust your spending habits and save money. How much of your monthly income could you save—5 percent? Great, let's start there. This year, commit to saving 5 percent (or whatever percent-age you decide) of your total earnings. Increase the amount by 1 percent of your earnings each year until you have reached your goal of saving, say, 10 percent or even more. You can also set goals regarding your net worth, especially if you plan to buy property. When you start your retirement savings, make it a goal to max out your allowable contributions. If you can't do so the first year, set and stick to a goal of when you will do it.

In five or so years, with such incremental increases in the amounts you save, you just might find yourself saving more money than you thought possible. Best of all, you are going to be excited about the balances in these accounts. I have found that getting out from under debt reinforces the desire not to repeat that cycle, and having money in the bank motivates you to save even more.

My Second Financial Advisor: My Father

As your financial portfolio becomes increasingly bigger and more complex, you will need the guidance and expertise of a financial advisor. Over the years, investment opportunities and vehicles will change, and you will need someone looking out for your fi-nancial best interests. Before I leave this chapter, I would like to recognize my second financial advisor, my father.

While it was my mother who told me to pay myself first, it was my father who put things into action. During the course of his life-time, he managed to put four children through college, purchase a home and a vacation home, and own two rental properties. In addi-tion, from the simplest forms of savings, he managed to grow a di-verse financial portfolio with a variety of investment vehicles. Much of this he did on his own and later in life. While he made a few mistakes and has a few financial regrets, what I have taken away most from his experiences, and what is now being mirrored in my life, is that you will learn as you grow and as your money grows.

While you are starting your financial process, you will work with checking and savings accounts. You will shop around for the best interest rates on credit cards and loans. You will move up to CDs, money market accounts, and IRAs, and eventually you'll start investing in stocks and bonds. As your money grows, so too will your expertise in managing your money. You do not need to know everything all at once. Knowledge and experience will come in good time.

Learn More

The Internet is a great place to learn more about the financial tools available to you. Compare banks and investment houses. Compare loan rates, and find helpful websites. A good place to start is the site for the Federal Citizen Information Center, www. pueblo.gsa.gov, which has some basic and useful information on a variety of financial matters. Much of this information is free or is available for a small fee, with a modest handling charge for information mailed to you.

For the most part, the principles of personal financial planning presented in this chapter are those everyone can use to help secure a financially sound future. However, having chosen a career as an actor, you must be particularly diligent about starting and maintaining a continuous investment regime. No one else is going to do it for you. Your reserve cash fund and the peace of mind that comes from saving for retirement will make you better prepared to face the challenges of your industry. Because you are prepared financially, you will be able to take advantage of opportunities that others may not have.

If I could say only one thing in this chapter, it would be this: You have to pay attention to your money as equally as you pay attention to your career. You need to be active in lowering your debt and increasing your interest earnings by taking advantage of certain investment tools. Saving money is one thing; having your money work for you is a totally different ball game.

Scaring You Straight to the Bank

I do not wish to be a doomsayer, and I do not wish to cripple anyone with fear, but signs out there indicate that things are getting tougher for everyone, and much of that is because people are failing to live within their means.

As I said earlier, Americans now save at a negative rate. That is, they spend more money than they take in. That borrowed money will have to be repaid some day. As reported by Jonathan Clements in *The Wall Street Journal*, retirees are feeling compelled to return to work, adult children are providing financial assistance to their parents, and people are borrowing more than ever to send their children to school (Clements 2006b). Clements states that expenses for homes and cars are taking up a bigger percentage of Americans' total spending. Why? Because lately a lot of people have forgotten about the financial truths and started spending money on things they did not need, and now they cannot go back. What is going to happen to them? Some of these people may have stretched themselves so thin that they might end up foreclosing on their homes, selling their cars, or, worse, not doing the things they really wanted to do in life. I imagine most will fare okay in the end, but what if they had been smarter with their money from the start rather than following trends and fads?

Over the past several years, we have heard much about the failing social security system and big corporations abandoning their pension programs. While politicians may use the social security issue as a way to drum up votes, I think we should take away this lesson: The system now in place will probably be altered in some manner in the future, and we should be prepared for that. We need to be able to take care of ourselves. We need to plan for our own future and our retirement. Whatever comes our way, we need to be prepared.

In an article for *The Wall Street Journal*, Jeff Opdyke suggests that saving 10 percent of your income is no longer sufficient for retirement (Opdyke 2006). Instead, he states that financial planners are beginning to suggest saving more than 15 percent of your annual income as a more suitable goal. And if you start late in building your retirement savings, you need to increase your contributions to an even higher percentage to catch up for lost time.

Saving for retirement seems to be a concept that people know about but avoid acting on. "A recent report by the nonprofit Employee Benefit Research Institute showed that a quarter of workers are 'very confident' about retirement security, even though twenty-two percent of them aren't currently saving and forty percent have less than $50,000 put aside" (Opdyke 2006, p. B1). The article also highlights the work of financial advisor Charles Farrell of Ohio, who uses a debt-to-savings ratio to determine fiscal well-being (Figure 5–5).

Ratio	30 Years Old	45 Years Old
Savings to Income	0.1 times Annual Salary	3 times Annual Salary
Debt to Income	1.7 times Annual Salary	Equal to Annual Salary
Retirement Savings Rate to Income	12% of Income	12% of Income

Figure 5–5   Debt-to-Savings Ratio (Source: Adapted from "Will You Be Able to Retire?" The Wall Street Journal, *Opdyke 2006, p. B1)*

Farrell suggests that as you begin your career, you should be less concerned about savings and more focused on debt control and reduction; however, as you get older, you should increase savings and further reduce debt. In other words, you should be increasing your net worth as you move through your career, not reducing it by taking on more debt.

However you look at it, you need to be saving for retirement now. The sooner you start, the better off you will be. Using the power of compound interest and long-term investment strategies is far better than trying to save money at the end of your professional career. Start planning for retirement, and make it a priority now!

What I like best about all of this is that it gives us goals to work for and achieve. How does your financial situation fit into Farrell's ratios? Are you doing better or worse? How can you adjust your behavior to begin to create a positive outlook for your future?

You are too important to leave your future up to chance.

Notes from the Field: When Should I Pay Attention to My Investment Strategy?

Your investment portfolio strategy should be revisited once a year with your financial advisor. The discussion should include conversation about how your life has changed since you last reviewed your investment strategy and what the advisor predicts the coming year will bring for the financial markets. Wholesale strategy changes are rarely warranted, though annual rebalancing of portfolios is generally a good idea. Rebalancing keeps extreme market moves from stretching your

continued

portfolio mix far away from your original strategy. Reputable advisors will rebalance your portfolio once or twice a year. More often is not necessary and is likely counterproductive to your wealth-building success.

Resist the temptation to buy or sell securities based on tips and emotions. Professional investors carefully monitor the investment activity of "odd lot" investors, that is, small investors, and often do exactly the opposite of what they see small investors doing. Find a competent financial advisor who uses professional investment portfolio managers on your behalf. You have a better chance of not coming late to the party.

—R. F.

Action Items

- Set goals for each area of your financial plan:
  - Paying off and managing bad debt
  - Establishing a cash reserve fund
  - Short-term savings
  - Long-term and retirement savings
- Pay off any bad debt.
- Shop for more favorable interest rates for your savings and your debt.
- Create a cash reserve fund.
- Investigate retirement savings options.
- Establish an IRA or other retirement fund account.
- Learn more about how to manage your money, and explore other investment opportunities.

6 Understanding Common Tax Laws

s Benjamin Franklin so famously said, "In this world nothing is certain but death and taxes." For many, tax time is an occasion of utter dread. It is the arduous task of filling out forms and shelling out money to the U.S. government. But it may not have to be so dreadful. Instead of thinking of tax laws as a way you're cheated out of your money, you might want to think of them as a way to get some of your money back. That's right, get some of it back! The U.S. government offers its citizens a number of tax breaks and deductions that reduce their taxable incomes and thus lower the taxes they pay. The trick is to be prepared for the big day—April 15—by having carefully recorded your spending throughout the year.

I recognize that this chapter will be difficult to understand and follow, especially for people who have never completed a tax form. My intention is not to cover every detail of the U.S. tax code but rather to give you an overview and to note some things to look out for. Tax laws change annually, and you need to keep abreast of changes that might be made since they could be helpful to your situation. While you read this chapter, you can refer to the tax forms included in the appendixes of this book or visit the Internal Revenue Service (IRS) website at www.irs.gov and find the forms and instructions for yourself, especially if you feel they pertain to your tax situation.

Understanding Common Tax Forms

The basic form everyone starts their tax filing with is Form 1040 (see Appendix A). There are two other variations: Form 1040EZ and Form 1040A. Generally, you can consider using the 1040EZ, which is a simpler form to complete than the 1040. You may use Form 1040EZ if your taxable income is less than $100,000 and you do not wish to claim any adjustments to your income. (However, after reading this chapter, you most certainly will want to claim deductions from your earned income.) People who take deductions must choose between Forms 1040 and 1040A. If your income is more than $100,000 at the end of the year, you are required to complete Form 1040. If you itemize your deductions and claim adjustments to your income other than educator expenses, IRA deductions, student loans, and tuition and fees, you will need to use Form 1040. Your level of income and the number of deductions you are taking will dictate which form to use. In this chapter, we will discuss Form 1040.

Income

We begin our discussion on the first page of Form 1040, lines 7 through 22, where you record your income (Figure 6–1). Several areas need to be covered in this section, including wages (line 7), business income (line 12), and unemployment compensation (line 19). However, before we continue, we must clarify the distinction between being an employee and being self-employed.

Income			
Attach Form(s) W-2 here. Also attach Forms W-2G and 1099-R if tax was withheld.	7	Wages, salaries, tips, etc. Attach Form(s) W-2	7
	8a	Taxable interest. Attach Schedule B if required	8a
	b	Tax-exempt interest. Do not include on line 8a 8b	
	9a	Ordinary dividends. Attach Schedule B if required	9a
	b	Qualified dividends (see page 23) 9b	
	10	Taxable refunds, credits, or offsets of state and local income taxes (see page 24) . .	10
	11	Alimony received	11
	12	Business income or (loss). Attach Schedule C or C-EZ	12
	13	Capital gain or (loss). Attach Schedule D if required. If not required, check here ▶ ☐	13
If you did not get a W-2, see page 23.	14	Other gains or (losses). Attach Form 4797	14
	15a	IRA distributions . . 15a	b Taxable amount (see page 25)	15b
	16a	Pensions and annuities 16a	b Taxable amount (see page 26)	16b
Enclose, but do not attach, any payment. Also, please use Form 1040-V.	17	Rental real estate, royalties, partnerships, S corporations, trusts, etc. Attach Schedule E	17
	18	Farm income or (loss). Attach Schedule F	18
	19	Unemployment compensation	19
	20a	Social security benefits 20a	b Taxable amount (see page 27)	20b
	21	Other income. List type and amount (see page 29)	21
	22	Add the amounts in the far right column for lines 7 through 21. This is your total income ▶	22

Figure 6–1   IRS Form 1040: Income

Employee versus Self-Employed As an actor, you will probably find yourself in both of these situations, sometimes working as an employee and sometimes being self-employed (also referred to as freelance or independent contractor work), which can be a good thing. As a salaried or wage-earning employee, you are usually paid on a regular, ongoing basis for the period of your contract. As an employee (e.g., a salaried actor in a show, an office worker), you will have a number of deductions taken from your paycheck, including federal and state taxes, social security, Federal Insurance Contributions Act (FICA) tax, and Medicare. At the beginning of the year (no later than January 31), for each job you worked you will receive a W-2 form stating your total earnings and deductions from those earnings.

Someone who is self-employed or an independent contractor enters into a contract agreement with an organization. A fee is provided to the contractor for services rendered. No taxes or other deductions are taken out of the fee; therefore, as an independent contractor, you are responsible for all tax obligations (line 58). If the amount paid to a given contractor during a year totals more than $600, the organization is required to send that contractor a 1099 Form indicating the total payment amount for the given tax year. The organization also reports this amount to the IRS.

Wages, Salaries, and Tips Line 7 of Form 1040 is where you begin to tally your yearly income. After receiving all of your W-2 forms from your employers, you can enter the total of your W-2 income on line 7. Also included on this line are the tips you received.

If you do not receive a W-2 from a previous employer, you should retrieve this information so that your filings are complete and accurate. It is a good idea to keep a running list of each employer you've had during the year. Keep a record of the address and phone number as well as the name of the person responsible for distributing W-2s and 1099s. If you move, you should let these companies know your new address so that there is no delay in receiving your tax information at the beginning of the year. It is also a good habit to keep your pay stubs from employers, just in case.

Business Income Line 12, for business income or loss, is where you record the net amount of money you earned as an independent contractor. To determine business income or loss, you are required to complete Schedule C (see Appendix C) or Schedule C-EZ. Again, your goal is to reduce your taxable income. You do this through Schedule C by subtracting your business expenses from your earnings.

Think of it like this: You are a business, and the 1099s represent your gross income. You had to spend money to run your business; these are business expenses. Your net income therefore is your gross income minus your business expenses. The government taxes you on your net income.

Schedule C Before we get into Schedule C, let's look at the total picture of why you are receiving 1099s and what services you provided. As an actor, you may be receiving 1099s for teaching classes, presenting at seminars, assisting directors, and so on, but you may have another job not related to theatre that also provides income. For example, let's say that you translate books to English from French. Since you perform this work at your own pace and in your own home, you are self-employed. Because you receive 1099s for two distinct businesses, you should complete two Schedule Cs, one for each business grouping. There is no tax benefit of separating them, but your financial picture will be clearer to you and the IRS.

There are five parts to Schedule C: Income, Expenses, Cost of Goods Sold, Information on Your Vehicle, and Other Expenses. Beginning with Part I, line 1, you enter your gross receipts (Figure 6–2). Gross receipts are the combined total of your 1099s, provided they are for the same business grouping.

In Part II, lines 8 through 27 are fairly straightforward and self-explanatory (Figure 6–3); these items are the expenses you

Figure 6–2 IRS Schedule C, Part I

Part II Expenses. Enter expenses for business use of your home **only** on line 30.

8	Advertising	8		18	Office expense	18
9	Car and truck expenses (see page C-4)	9		19	Pension and profit-sharing plans	19
10	Commissions and fees	10		20	Rent or lease (see page C-5):	
11	Contract labor (see page C-4)	11		a	Vehicles, machinery, and equipment	20a
12	Depletion	12		b	Other business property	20b
13	Depreciation and section 179 expense deduction (not included in Part III) (see page C-4)	13		21	Repairs and maintenance	21
				22	Supplies (not included in Part III)	22
				23	Taxes and licenses	23
				24	Travel, meals, and entertainment:	
				a	Travel	24a
14	Employee benefit programs (other than on line 19)	14		b	Deductible meals and entertainment (see page C-6)	24b
15	Insurance (other than health)	15		25	Utilities	25
16	Interest:			26	Wages (less employment credits)	26
a	Mortgage (paid to banks, etc.)	16a		27	Other expenses (from line 48 on page 2)	27
b	Other	16b				
17	Legal and professional services	17				

28 Total expenses before expenses for business use of home. Add lines 8 through 27 in columns ▶ **28**

29 Tentative profit (loss). Subtract line 28 from line 7 **29**
30 Expenses for business use of your home. Attach Form 8829 **30**
31 Net profit or (loss). Subtract line 30 from line 29.
• If a profit, enter on both **Form 1040, line 12,** and **Schedule SE, line 2,** or on **Form 1040NR, line 13** (statutory employees, see page C-6). Estates and trusts, enter on Form 1041, line 3. **31**
• If a loss, you **must** go to line 32.
32 If you have a loss, check the box that describes your investment in this activity (see page C-6).
• If you checked 32a, enter the loss on both **Form 1040, line 12,** and **Schedule SE, line 2,** or on **Form 1040NR, line 13** (statutory employees, see page C-6). Estates and trusts, enter on Form 1041, line 3.
• If you checked 32b, you **must** attach **Form 6198.** Your loss may be limited.
32a ☐ All investment is at risk.
32b ☐ Some investment is not at risk.

For Paperwork Reduction Act Notice, see page C-8 of the instructions. Cat. No. 11334P Schedule C (Form 1040) 2006

Figure 6–3 IRS Schedule C, Part II

may have encountered in the day-to-day operation of your business. These expenses include advertising, legal and professional services, office expense, rent, repairs, supplies, tax and licenses, travel, meals, entertainment, and utilities.

Part III is for a business that produces physical products to sell, so you will most likely not need to fill out that section. Part IV covers business usage of your vehicle. The final section, Part V, is a place to note expenses not covered in Part II.

Subtracting your total expenses from your gross earnings will provide you with your net income, the amount taxed by the U.S. government. Therefore, it is to your advantage to keep track of all your business expenses and record them within Schedule C.

Self-Employment Tax Just because you are an independent contractor does not mean you can escape from paying taxes. Persons who record net income on their Schedule C forms must pay taxes on that profit by completing Schedule SE. For earnings of $90,000 or less, multiply your net income by 15.3 percent, which determines your self-employment tax—the amount you should pay to cover your portion of social security and Medicare taxes. Enter this number on line 58 of Form 1040. You can also deduct one-half of that amount from your adjusted gross income on line 27 of the same form. Reducing your net income will help reduce your self-employment tax, so it's another reason to record all of your business expenses.

Estimated Tax Payments Being self-employed can have many advantages; however, if you're not careful, you can end the year with a serious IOU to the government. If you have earned a consistent (more than one year) and substantial amount of your earnings through self-employment, you should file quarterly estimated taxes. If you find yourself in this situation, it would be advisable to seek professional help in preparing your quarterly filings.

Adjusted Gross Income

After calculating your yearly earnings, you focus again on reducing your taxable income through the next section of Form 1040: Adjusted Gross Income, lines 23 through 37 (Figure 6–4). In this section, found at the bottom of the first page of the 1040, are three deductions that many people might be eligible for regardless of profession. Let's discuss each of those next.

	22	Add the amounts in the far right column for lines 7 through 21. This is your total income ►	22	
Adjusted Gross Income	23	Archer MSA deduction. Attach Form 8853	23	
	24	Certain business expenses of reservists, performing artists, and fee-basis government officials. Attach Form 2106 or 2106-EZ	24	
	25	Health savings account deduction. Attach Form 8889 . .	25	
	26	Moving expenses. Attach Form 3903	26	
	27	One-half of self-employment tax. Attach Schedule SE . .	27	
	28	Self-employed SEP, SIMPLE, and qualified plans . . .	28	
	29	Self-employed health insurance deduction (see page 29)	29	
	30	Penalty on early withdrawal of savings	30	
	31a	Alimony paid b Recipient's SSN ►	31a	
	32	IRA deduction (see page 31)	32	
	33	Student loan interest deduction (see page 33)	33	
	34	Jury duty pay you gave to your employer	34	
	35	Domestic production activities deduction. Attach Form 8903	35	
	36	Add lines 23 through 31a and 32 through 35	36	
	37	Subtract line 36 from line 22. This is your **adjusted gross income** . . . . . ►	37	

For Disclosure, Privacy Act, and Paperwork Reduction Act Notice, see page 80.   Cat. No. 11320B   Form **1040** (2006)

Figure 6–4 IRS Form 1040: Adjusted Gross Income

Depending on your personal situation, you might be able to make other adjustments in the Adjusted Gross Income section, including those for certain business expenses (line 24), health savings accounts (line 25), one-half of your self-employment tax (line 26), self-employed retirement contributions and health insurance (lines 28 and 29), alimony payments (line 31), and IRA accounts (line 32).

Moving Expenses The deduction for moving expenses appears on line 26. If you move because of a job, you may be eligible to deduct certain expenses related to that move. There are two tests when considering eligibility for this deduction. First, is the new job more than fifty miles further from your former home? That is, if your former job was ten miles away from your former home, your new job has to be at least sixty miles away from your former residence. The second test is that of time. According to the IRS website, "If you are an employee, you must work full time for at least 39 weeks during the 12 months right after you move. If you are self-employed, you must work full time for at least 39 weeks during the first 12 months and for a total of at least 78 weeks during the first 24 months after you move" (Internal Revenue Service 2005). If you meet these requirements, you will need to complete Form 3903.

Penalty for Early Withdrawal of Savings If during the previous year you found yourself in a financial pinch, needed to withdraw money from certain long-term savings accounts, and were charged a penalty for the withdrawal, you can deduct that fee from your taxable income. If this is the case, you should receive a Form 1099-INT or Form 1099-OID indicating the amount you were charged. You can enter that number on line 30 of Form 1040. It is a good idea to keep an ongoing record of these penalties with your other tax records.

Student Loan Interest Deduction Anyone who went to college and is paying back a student loan can use this deduction. Although some restrictions do apply, in general you can deduct up to $2,500 of interest paid on student loans. Typically, your lender will send you a statement indicating the amount of interest you paid during the year. Enter that amount (up to $2,500) on line 33.

Tuition and Fees Deductions

If you are currently taking classes at a college or university, you may be able to deduct a portion of these expenses. This will get a little tricky. First we must make a distinction between a tax deduction and a tax credit.

Tax Deductions and Tax Credits

A *tax deduction* directly reduces your taxable income. For example, if you earn $50,000 in a year and you take a deduction of $2,500 for student loan interest, your taxable income is $47,500. Your taxes will be lower as a result, but they will not be $2,500 lower. A *tax credit* directly reduces the amount of taxes you owe. For example, if you owe $5,200 in taxes but then take a tax credit of $2,000, you end up owing only $3,200. Every dollar of a tax credit you can take reduces your taxes by a dollar. It is therefore to your advantage to take tax credits rather than deductions, although we will take whatever we can get.

Tuition and Fees Deduction

If your total income is too high to be eligible for the Hope Credit or the Lifetime Learning Credit, you may be able to take advantage of this deduction reducing your taxable income up to $4,000. It is important to note that this deduction was scheduled to expire in 2005 but has been extended through 2007. After 2007 you should check with the IRS to see if this deduction is available. IRS Publication 970 explains all of the possible deductions and credits one may take advantage of when filing their taxes. If you qualify for the Tuition and Fees Deduction, you may do so on Line 35 of the 1040 Form—Domestic Production Activities—by entering "T" for tuition and fees.

Education Tax Credit

To be eligible for an education tax credit (line 50), you must have paid money for you, your spouse, or your dependent to attend an institution of higher education. You may not be able to take this credit and thus may be eligible only for a tax deduction on line 33 if your adjusted gross income (line 38) is more than $53,000 for an individual or $107,000 if married and filing jointly.

The Hope Credit versus the Lifetime Learning Credit There are two categories for educational credit: the Hope Credit and the Lifetime Learning Credit. The first is more restrictive and applies only toward the first two years of education after high school. However, if you qualify, you can take a credit of up to $1,500 per student. Through the Lifetime Learning Credit, you can qualify for a credit of up to $2,000 per return.

The U.S. government offers a number of options when accounting for educational expenses. Before determining the type of deduction or credit to take, make certain that you have explored all of your options and have obtained the highest possible tax benefit.

Tax and Credits

Moving to the second page of Form 1040, we come to the Tax and Credits section (Figure 6–5). In the first part of this section, you will determine whether it is best for you to take the standard deduction or to itemize your deductions. This along with other deductions will determine your taxable income (line 43) and your tax amount prior to credits (line 44). Once you have determined

Form 1040 (2006) Page 2

Tax and Credits

Standard Deduction for—
- People who checked any box on line 39a or 39b or who can be claimed as a dependent, see page 34.
- All others:

Single or Married filing separately, $5,150

Married filing jointly or Qualifying widow(er), $10,300

Head of household, $7,550

38	Amount from line 37 (adjusted gross income)	38
39a	Check if: ☐ **You** were born before January 2, 1942, ☐ Blind. ☐ **Spouse** was born before January 2, 1942, ☐ Blind. Total boxes checked ▶ 39a ☐	
b	If your spouse itemizes on a separate return or you were a dual-status alien, see page 34 and check here ▶39b ☐	
40	**Itemized deductions** (from Schedule A) **or** your **standard deduction** (see left margin)	40
41	Subtract line 40 from line 38	41
42	If line 38 is over $112,875, or you provided housing to a person displaced by Hurricane Katrina, see page 36. Otherwise, multiply $3,300 by the total number of exemptions claimed on line 6d	42
43	**Taxable income.** Subtract line 42 from line 41. If line 42 is more than line 41, enter -0-	43
44	Tax (see page 36). Check if any tax is from: a ☐ Form(s) 8814 b ☐ Form 4972	44
45	**Alternative minimum tax** (see page 39). Attach Form 6251	45
46	Add lines 44 and 45 ▶	46
47	Foreign tax credit. Attach Form 1116 if required	47
48	Credit for child and dependent care expenses. Attach Form 2441	48
49	Credit for the elderly or the disabled. Attach Schedule R	49
50	Education credits. Attach Form 8863	50
51	Retirement savings contributions credit. Attach Form 8880	51
52	Residential energy credits. Attach Form 5695	52
53	Child tax credit (see page 42). Attach Form 8901 if required	53
54	Credits from: a ☐ Form 8396 b ☐ Form 8839 c ☐ Form 8859	54
55	Other credits: a ☐ Form 3800 b ☐ Form 8801 c ☐ Form____	55
56	Add lines 47 through 55. These are your **total credits**	56
57	Subtract line 56 from line 46. If line 56 is more than line 46, enter -0- ▶	57

Figure 6–5 IRS Form 1040: Tax and Credits

your tax, you can apply credits directly to that amount, lowering the total you owe.

Let's walk through an example of what is meant by a tax credit on page 2 of Form 1040 and a deduction on page 1. We'll say that you're married and your adjusted gross income on line 37 is $50,000. You take the standard deduction for a married couple filing jointly of $10,300, reducing your taxable income to $39,700. On line 42 you then further reduce this number by $9,900 by claiming three exemptions: you, your wife, and your child. This leaves you with your taxable income (line 43) and your tax due (line 44). From the 2006 tax table, the amount of taxes you would owe on $29,800 is $3,719.

In the following section, lines 47 through 55, you directly reduce the tax amount you owe by taking advantage of credits. We already discussed the education credit (line 50), but you may also be able to take credits for retirement savings and childcare, as well as the child tax credit. Again, based on your personal situation, you may be able to take advantage of other credits found in this section.

If you take an education credit of $1,500, your tax due would be $2,219. If, however, you instead take the deduction on page 1, line 35, your adjusted gross income on line 37 would be $48,500. All other things remaining the same, your taxes due would be $3,494 on $28,300. You can save some money in taxes if you can take a credit instead of a deduction.

Credit for Child and Dependent Care Expenses

If you have a child or are responsible for a disabled person who cannot care for him- or herself and you pay for help (e.g., day care) while you work, you may be eligible to receive a tax credit for this expense. You will need to use Form 2441 to determine eligibility and the amount of credit.

Retirement Savings

If you made contributions throughout the year to a traditional IRA, a Roth IRA, or SEP, SIMPLE, or other employee retirement plans, you may be eligible to receive a credit for that amount. However, restrictions do apply. You cannot take this credit if your adjusted gross income was more than $25,000 for an individual and $50,000 if you are filing jointly. Also, you are not eligible if you were born after January 1, 1988, or were enrolled as a student during the tax year.

Itemized Deductions

On the first page of Form 1040, you calculated your adjusted gross income (line 37): your earnings minus deductions. That was fairly straightforward. The examples given for page 2, Tax and Credits section, covered an individual who elected to use the standard deduction amount as dictated by the IRS. However, one may choose to itemize their deductions. It is in this section that you need to determine whether to use the standard deduction or to itemize your deductions.

Itemized versus Standard Deductions

Individuals can either itemize their deductions or use the standard deduction allowed by the IRS. For individual filers, the standard deduction is $5,150 for the 2006 tax year. This deduction directly reduces your adjusted taxable income. Therefore, you should use the itemization option only if your itemized deductions amount to more than the standard deduction, in this case, $5,150. As a general rule, when doing my taxes, I go through the itemizing process to ensure I am taking full advantage of all tax options. This also helps make me aware of the types of things I should pay attention to throughout the coming year.

Itemizing Deductions

If you are itemizing deductions, you will need to use Schedule A (see Appendix B). Schedule A records an individual's medical and dental expenses, taxes paid, interest paid, gifts to charities, casualties or theft losses, job expenses, and other miscellaneous deductions. These are explained more fully below.

Medical and Dental Expenses   In today's climate of soaring medical and insurance costs, this deduction (Figure 6–6) has the potential to save you money, especially if you pay for your own medical insurance or have gone without it. Under this deduction, you can

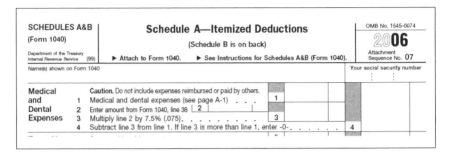

Figure 6–6   IRS Schedule A: Medical and Dental Expenses

claim your insurance premiums, dental exams, prescriptions, and eye care. Any expense related to your health has the potential for deduction. Even if you are covered by an employee plan, you can still claim copayments and any other out-of-pocket expenses you may incur. However, the rule is that you may deduct only those medical expenses that exceed 7.5 percent of your adjusted gross income (line 37). As an example, if your adjusted gross income is $47,250, you need to have medical expenses in excess of $3,544. Any amount above that level you may use to itemize your deductions. In general, you would take this deduction if you had a major medical procedure or incurred exceptionally high prescription costs.

Taxes You Paid   The next section of Schedule A documents taxes you paid during the tax year (Figure 6–7). These include federal taxes, social security, and unemployment taxes found on your W-2 form(s). You may also deduct state income or sales taxes on major purchases. Lines 6 and 7 allow you to deduct real estate and

Taxes You Paid				
(See page A-3.)	5	State and local income taxes	5	
	6	Real estate taxes (see page A-3)	6	
	7	Personal property taxes	7	
	8	Other taxes. List type and amount ▶	8	
	9	Add lines 5 through 8		9

Figure 6–7   IRS Schedule A: Taxes You Paid

property taxes, which may be valuable if you own a home or property. This is a fairly complicated section of Schedule A, and I will not attempt to summarize it. You should be aware that if you plan to itemize your deductions, you can include state and local taxes paid in that year. You should consult the IRS on what you can deduct and how to properly file those deductions using Schedule A.

Interest You Paid   For people who own a home, this section is of particular importance (Figure 6–8). In this portion of Schedule A, you may be able to deduct interest you paid toward your mortgage as well as other investment interest payments. Of course, as in other sections, certain rules and restrictions apply, and you should carefully read and understand your options.

Gifts to Charities   As an actor, you will probably associate with some nonprofit organizations and become familiar with the practice of making charitable contributions. In this section (Figure 6–9), you can claim gifts to charities that you made in cash or through

Interest You Paid (See page A-3.)	10	Home mortgage interest and points reported to you on Form 1098	10	
	11	Home mortgage interest not reported to you on Form 1098. If paid to the person from whom you bought the home, see page A-3 and show that person's name, identifying no., and address ▶	11	
Note. Personal interest is not deductible.	12	Points not reported to you on Form 1098. See page A-4 for special rules	12	
	13	Investment interest. Attach Form 4952 if required. (See page A-4.)	13	
	14	Add lines 10 through 13		14

Figure 6–8   IRS Schedule A: Interest You Paid

Gifts to Charity If you made a gift and got a benefit for it, see page A-4.	15	Gifts by cash or check. If you made any gift of $250 or more, see page A-5	15	
	16	Other than by cash or check. If any gift of $250 or more, see page A-5. You must attach Form 8283 if over $500	16	
	17	Carryover from prior year	17	
	18	Add lines 15 through 17		18

Figure 6–9   IRS Schedule A: Gifts to Charities

property (e.g., a car, clothing). You may also deduct out-of-pocket expenses you paid in order to fulfill volunteer work (e.g., if you volunteered for a theatre and had to pay for parking your car). If your contribution was $250 or more, you should receive confirmation of that gift from the charitable organization, although most organizations do this as standard practice regardless of the size of the gift. Any gifts of property you contributed can be deducted based on their fair market value at the time of the donation.

Casualty and Theft Losses   I've always thought that this was a very compassionate section of Schedule A. In this section, you can complete Form 4684 to determine your deductions for losses incurred through theft, vandalism, fire, storm, and/or other accidents. Obviously, you cannot claim this deduction if you were reimbursed through an insurance provider. However, if you do not have insurance or your insurance did not cover all of the loss or damage, this section may help you recover a portion of your losses.

Job Expenses and Miscellaneous Deductions   Many of us spend our own money for things we do for work. Sometimes the company does not reimburse us for these expenses. In such cases, we might consider deducting them from our taxes. Schedule A is one place to do so (Figure 6–10). Similar to the rule for itemizing medical costs, you can begin to account for nonreimbursed job expenses only if they're greater than 2 percent of your adjusted gross income. So if your adjusted gross income is $47,250, you cannot claim the first 2 percent or $945 of nonreimbursed business expenses.

Figure 6–10   IRS Schedule A: Job Expenses and Miscellaneous Deductions

Be Prepared

For someone who does not own a home or other real estate, itemizing deductions is not usually to his or her advantage because itemizing totals are usually less than the standard deduction. However, should something extraordinary (e.g., a stay at the hospital, a robbery at your apartment, storm damage, and so on) happen to you in a given year, you should be prepared to take advantage of the tax opportunity.

For example, let's say that you become ill and need to be hospitalized. While you do have health insurance, your copay is high, and you have to pay approximately $5,000 for this illness. This places you in the realm of itemization. Combined with all your other possible deductions, you may find more benefits in itemizing your deductions than taking the standard deduction, even if you didn't itemize last year. It is a matter of being prepared for any situation. In this way, you get more of your money back. You reduce your tax amount at a time when you really need every dollar.

Keeping Proper Records

Having just begun to scratch the surface with regard to personal taxes, one thing is clear: You need to keep track of all your activities in order to take greatest advantage of certain parts of the tax code. The IRS gives tax deductions and credits for many common transactions, but people fail to take advantage of them through a lack of either knowledge or preparedness. At first it will seem like a lot of work to track all of the items that might apply to your tax filings. But like most things, after you do it for a while, it will become second nature to you. And remember, these little acts might save you some money.

Likewise, once you file your tax forms, you should retain these records. You can use them to track your progress and to show the IRS should you be audited. You need keep only the records that pertain to your filings.

The IRS does have a very good website (www.irs.gov), where you can download forms and instructions. It is also a place to find answers to some of your tax questions. With a little research, you can find what you need.

Action Items

- Collect and store your previous tax returns in one place.
- Review the IRS forms and website at www.irs.gov.
- Create a filing system for records related to possible tax deductions.
- Create a filing system for employer contracts and pay stubs.
- Save your receipts!

◤◢ Taxes and the Actor

Now that you have a basic understanding of common tax code, this chapter will focus on the business of acting and on particular issues regarding your personal tax filings. Certain rules that apply to the performing arts industry can save you money, provided that you qualify, of course.

Qualified Performing Artists

In 1986, a provision was included in the tax code known as Qualified Performing Artist (QPA). This provision is explained in the IRS's Instructions for Form 2106, although it is fairly straightforward.

> If you are a qualified performing artist, you can deduct your employee business expenses as an adjustment to income rather than as a miscellaneous itemized deduction. To qualify, you must meet all three of the following requirements.
>
> 1. You perform services in the performing arts for at least two employers during your tax year. (You are considered to have performed services in the performing arts for an employer only if that employer paid you $200 or more.)
> 2. Your allowable business expenses related to the performing arts are more than 10% of your gross income from the performing arts.

3. Your adjusted gross income is not more than $16,000 before deducting these business expenses.

If you do not meet all of the above requirements, you must deduct your expenses as a miscellaneous itemized deduction subject to the 2% limit. (Internal Revenue Service 2005)

This can be a bit confusing, so let's consider a real-life example. Say that for the past tax year you earned $7,000 as an actor through contracts with six companies, and therefore you meet the first requirement of the QPA provision. If any of the $7,000 was paid to you as an independent contractor (i.e., you were self-employed), you would list those earnings and the related expenses on Schedule C. Those business expenses cannot be claimed again under QPA. For this example, let's say that all of the $7,000 was paid to you as an employee—you received regular payments, and taxes were taken out of your salary.

Now we move to the next stipulation: Your QPA expenses must be more than 10 percent of your QPA income. In our example, in order to deduct expenses, you must have receipts that total more than $700 (10 percent of $7,000). Let's say that you meet this requirement. A new batch of headshots from a quality photographer would take care of that amount rather quickly.

Finally, we come to the third provision, which states that in order to qualify for this deduction, your adjusted gross income (line 37 of IRS Form 1040) must be no more than $16,000 before you take this deduction. In other words, you have to complete the first page of your Form 1040, including all earnings and deductions. When you reach line 37, the last line on the first page, if that number is less than $16,000, you can go back to line 24, complete a Form 2106 or 2106-EZ, and enter your amount as a QPA deduction. If you qualify, you will have to go back to line 36 and recalculate your total deductions (lines 23 through 35) and then subtract that amount from line 22—total income—to give you a new and reduced adjusted gross income.

If you fail to meet the QPA requirements, you can try again to deduct your expenses by using Schedule A and itemizing your deductions rather than taking the standard deduction. Remember, under this scenario your itemized deductions must be greater than the standard deduction for you to create a tax benefit for yourself. If you do not make it this year, keep saving those receipts and keep trying. At some point, you may save yourself some money.

On September 14, 2006, a bill was introduced by Senator Charles Schumer of New York calling for changes in the QPA deductions, to increase the total earnings requirement from $16,000 to $30,000 and to adjust it for inflation thereafter. The bill was referred to the Committee on Finance. If the bill passes, it will help many young actors throughout the country. Keep your eye out for this possible change, and keep checking with the IRS before filing your 2007 tax forms.

Deductions for Actors

Your tax preparation does not begin when you start receiving your 1099s and W-2s; it begins on January 1 of each year. Knowing what to look for and what records to keep is most of the battle. Remember, you cannot deduct expenses from your income unless you have records of them. Keeping records does not mean simply having a shoebox full of receipts at the end of the year; rather, you should have an organized and complete list of your business transactions and should know why each of these transactions occurred. Here is a list of transactions that may be deductible under IRS regulations.

In Town Expenses
- Photos & Resumes
- Agent's/Manager's Commissions
- Union Dues/Initiation Fees
- Office Supplies/Stationery/Postage
- Business Phone Expenses
- Academy & Players Guide
- Accompanist/Audition Expense
- Answering Service
- Coaching/Lessons for Performance
- Entertainment for Business
- Gifts for Business
- Sheet music, Records, Books, Tapes
- Rehearsal clothes & Maintenance
- Tickets for Professional Research

- Trade Publications
- Transportation Seeking Employment

Out of Town Expenses
- Travel for jobs or job searches
- Lodging
- Meals
- Laundry & Dry Cleaning
- Local Transportation
- Auto (Business Rental)
- Gasoline/Auto Repairs & Maintenance
- Telephone Charges
- Tips & Gratuities
- Other Related Expenses

(Actors' Equity Association 2006a)

The personal and professional lives of an actor are so intertwined that they often feel one and the same: We are what we do. Because of this, it is often difficult to categorize the personal and professional expenses we encounter on a daily basis. But when in doubt, save the receipt and write on the back the reason for your purchase. Is it for a particular job you are working on? Is the expense related to finding future employment? Does it involve maintaining your skills, status, or image? If so, it is deductible, and you can use it to reduce your taxes.

Notes from the Field: Why Join Equity?

I've been asked many, many times, "Why should I join Equity?" Short answer: Because Equity has your back. Most performers would like to just work. It's really hard to sit down and figure out how much you are worth. Because frankly, actors would act whether they got paid or didn't get paid. In order to help you, the actor, Actors' Equity Association (AEA or Equity) was formed in 1913. It wasn't unusual for actors to be stranded in towns where shows closed. The actors were given no form of transportation, aid, or help of any kind. As a member of AEA, you will be fairly compensated for your work and saved from difficulties regarding your payment.

—D. C.

Preparing Your Taxes

The good news in all of this is that you have a few options when it comes to preparing your taxes. You can prepare them yourself with or without the assistance of tax software, you can use a service such as H&R Block, or you can hire a professional tax accountant who specializes in the entertainment industry. Equity offers a tax assistance program to its members as well. Obviously, as you move further up the ladder, expenses and fees for service increase, which should lead you to ask: Are you getting your money's worth? Determining what level of tax assistance you should seek is a matter of the complexity of your tax situation and your understanding of it.

As an actor, you have special conditions available to you with regard to deductibles. However, I believe that, at least in the beginning of your career, you should be able to handle your tax preparation on your own. I encourage this because you learn as you prepare your own taxes, and each year you are better prepared to take advantage of certain tax laws and codes. In this case, knowledge is more than power; knowledge can mean money in your pocket.

Tax Preparation Software

Over the past several years, I have used Intuit's TurboTax software to assist me with my personal and professional tax preparation. While I am not able to take many of the traditional deductions of ordinary home-owning taxpayers, I usually have earnings from a variety of sources and well as expenses that can be attributed to them. Generally, I have been happy with the results, especially since with Intuit's deluxe package, my state filing forms are also included.

As an experiment for this book, I compared TurboTax with H&R Block's TaxCut software, using the deluxe version from each company. Both contain federal and state filing information and forms. Although they are comparable packages (on the outside), I paid $10 more for TurboTax.

Both of the programs were easy to load and update. Each program checks for tax information updates every time you open the program. If you use financial software such as Quicken, Microsoft Money, or QuickBooks, you may import information from those programs. (I do not use these programs for my personal finances.) Both programs include sections for QPA deductions.

Both software packages gave me exactly the same results not only for my federal return but also for my state return. While both programs are very easy to use, I did like TurboTax slightly better—probably because I had used it in the past and was more familiar with it, but also because the sequence of tax questions seemed to make more sense and seemed a bit more thorough than TaxCut. However, I recommend both products as an easy way to help you through your taxes.

The great thing about these types of programs is that they complete all the tax forms you will need for your federal and state filings. By answering the questions step by step and being organized, you can indeed complete your taxes in a painless way. Doing it yourself also teaches you what you should look out for during the next tax year. I do feel that a certain understanding of the tax system helps me navigate the programs, but much of this I learned from the programs themselves.

The W-4 Form

Each time you are hired for an employee position, you have a tax decision to make. I am sure you have filled out this form a few times already yourself: the W-4 form. This form tells your employer how much federal tax to take out of your paycheck. Similar forms exist for state taxes. These forms are not checked by any official authority, so you can pretty much fill in whatever number of allowances you like. But what you claim will have an impact on your tax filing and what you do or do not owe come April 15.

Generally speaking, a typical single person can claim zero, one, or two personal allowances (Figure 7–1). If you claim zero allowances, the government is taking out the most taxes, and at the end of the year you will probably get some money back, provided you do not have income from other sources as an independent contractor. If you claim one allowance, you might have to pay a little in taxes when you file your annual tax forms, or you might get a little refund. If you claim two allowances, you can expect to pay taxes on April 15 because you have not had enough taken from your earnings throughout the year.

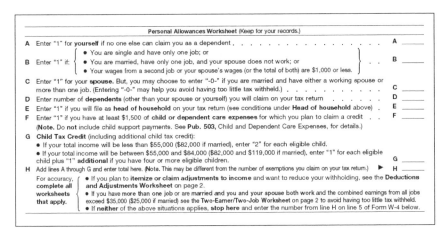

Figure 7–1   Personal Allowances Worksheet

If you have self-employment income in addition to salaries or wages as an employee, filling out a W-4 gets a little more complicated. As a contracted employee, you are required to state your earnings for these jobs and pay taxes on that income. If you know that you will be paid on a fee basis sometime in the tax year, you may claim zero allowances on your W-4 to help cover anticipated self-employment tax. I have known more than a few people who have been surprised to learn that they owe money from work they fulfilled as independent contractors.

Some people don't like to lend Uncle Sam their money throughout the year, so they claim as many allowances as possible. This is okay, too. But if you do this, I recommend that you save money throughout the year in preparation for your April tax bill.

Action Items

- Review your spending in relationship to allowable deductions.
- Review your current W-4 form(s) and adjust as necessary.
- Investigate the available tax software programs.

8 Other Important Information to Consider

When you are in the position to count your pennies, there are many ways you can save a few dollars here and there, and they begin to add up quickly. Regardless of how much money you make you should never be embarrassed about spending your money wisely. In this chapter, we will discuss several ideas for getting the most out of the money you do spend.

Notes from the Field: How I Got My Equity Card

I was a reader for auditions. What is a reader? Well, a reader is hired by the casting director to read with the actors who are auditioning for certain parts. A reader is expected to read all of the parts the actor is not auditioning for. I was lucky enough to be hired by Simon and Kumin casting, and I was reading for Doug Hughes, a director who was casting *Fables for Friends* at Playwrights Horizons. I worked as a reader for about two weeks, the show was cast, and I was hired to be a reader for another project. Before *Fables for Friends* opened, an actress had to leave the show. There wasn't any time to go through another round of auditions, so Doug Hughes asked if I was willing to join the cast because I was familiar with the play. I was delighted and said, "Yes, of course." I quickly learned the lines and blocking and was put in the show before it opened. I had to join Actors' Equity Association. So my entire paycheck went to Equity to pay for my membership fees and dues. That's how I got my card.

As a quick aside, I don't think you should ever read your reviews until six weeks after the show is closed. The atmosphere in the dressing room will tell you whether the reviews were positive or negative. But if you read specifics about your performance, you are just going to spend the remainder of the show thinking about the reviews and proving that the critics were wrong or proving that they were right. So, reading the reviews is going to affect your performance. I don't recommend you do it.

I went on to continue my education at New York University, and I was a founding member of Manhattan Class Company (MCC). We all founded that theater company so we could get work. Because even though I was a member of Equity, I still didn't have an agent, so I wasn't going out on many auditions. So, when we founded MCC, it gave us the equivalent of an "actor's gym." I was able to network, see plays, and perform. I did finally get an agent, and I worked pretty consistently regionally and in New York City. I never had to worry about asking for a certain amount in salary because, as a member of the union, my salary was standard.

Today there are a lot of ways to join Actors' Equity Association, especially the Equity Membership Candidate Program (EMC). Equity has tons of information, and you can get your questions answered by going to the website at www.actorsequity.org.

—D. C.

Unemployment Compensation

One option you may have as an actor in order to make ends meet during difficult times is collecting unemployment insurance from the state in which you reside. This book cannot cover every detail about filing for and collecting unemployment benefits because each state has different rules and regulations. Some of the typical questions to consider are these: What is the process of filing for unemployment compensation in your state? How much will you receive in benefits? How long will these benefits last? The good news is that states now have much of this information readily available online. Many states also allow you to sign up for benefits online, taking much of the dread and hassle out of the process.

An article on Monster.com reports, "Most states set a few additional rules regarding who can collect unemployment insurance.

First, you have to have worked for a certain amount of time, typically about a year and a half. Second, you have to be laid off—not fired—and you have to be in a covered position" (Aaron 2006).

You may also be eligible to receive unemployment compensation at the end of a contract, including contracts for acting. How much you receive is based on your prior earnings typically around 50 percent of your average weekly salary, and you may be eligible to receive these benefits for up to twenty-six weeks. However, you need to plan for the fact that unemployment compensation is subject to state and federal taxes. If you do not have some taxes withheld from each unemployment check, you could end up with a hefty tax bill on April 15. While unemployment compensation can be a viable alternative for supplementing your income between jobs, it is important to consider all of the pros and cons.

Bank Service Charges and Fees

Pull out your last bank statement, and take a look at how much money—your money—the bank charged you for using its services. Are these fees really necessary? I do not think so.

A bank may charge you to maintain checking or savings accounts or may require a minimum balance, it may charge for checks you write, and of course we all know about ATM fees. How do you avoid these charges? Tell your bank that you do not want to pay for those services anymore! One way you might be able to avoid fees and charges is by using direct deposit for your paychecks. You will need to check with your employer to see if this option is available to you. You can also shop around to find a bank that does not charge fees on its accounts or, in the worst-case scenario, that has a low minimum balance requirement—one that you know you can maintain.

As for ATM fees, the best way to get around them is to stop using other banks' ATMs. A typical ATM transaction using another bank costs you up to $4! You lose money every time you take money out of your account. If you find yourself constantly in this situation, you need to switch to the bank whose ATMs you use the most.

Shop around for a bank that has no-fee accounts and ATMs that are convenient to your everyday living. It should not cost you money to have a banking account. Sure, there will be occasions when you have to use another bank's machine, but this should happen only when you are out of town. Because actors tend to travel, you might consider banking at a large national or even international financial institution. This way, when you travel, you will have a much better chance that a branch of your bank will be available to you so you can avoid ATM fees.

Credit Cards

One of the great things about the Internet is that you can get a lot of good information about money matters. This is particularly true with credit cards. A website that I have used is www.bankrate.com. This site compares credit cards so you can see whether you are getting the best deal.

There are three major factors to consider when choosing a credit card: the interest rate (lower is better), the annual fee (free is best), and the grace period (the time between the purchase date and the date the company starts calculating interest). You may take advantage of low- or no-interest introductory offers from credit card companies, but you need to make sure you will have a fair interest rate once an offer has expired. Always read the fine print before signing up. Like all things, if it sounds too good to be true, it probably is. Many companies charge late fees and increase the interest rate on delinquent accounts. You can always call your credit card company and request a lower rate—it never hurts to ask.

Standard Monthly Bills

We all have them—phone bills, cable bills, loan payments, insurance premiums—but are we paying too much for them? In Chapter 4, you investigated your monthly spending habits. Here are a few quick things to think about regarding common monthly bills.

- Cell phones: The best advice when it comes to cell phones is to pay for exactly what you use, no more and no less. If you have a huge monthly service fee and aren't using the features you are paying for, you are losing money. Likewise, if you have a low monthly fee but are being charged for extra minutes or other charges, you probably need to upgrade your service.

- Land-line telephones: Many people today are deciding to forgo land-line telephones in their homes. If you are not willing to go that far, consider getting the most basic local calling plan.

- Internet services: There are many options available to consumers these days, including dial-up, DSL, and cable Internet access. Of course, each has a price. Depending on your Internet usage, you may consider downgrading your service to save a bit of money. You may also see if free wireless connection is available to you. Many cities and libraries are beginning to offer such services.

- Cable television: As with your cell phone service plan, with cable television you should pay only for what you use. Paying for a premium subscription you rarely or never watch is probably a waste of your money. With all the cheap movie rental options now available, you may want to pull the cable plug altogether.

- Car loans: Remember that car loans are like mortgages. First, you can refinance your car loan if you can obtain a better rate. There are many people willing to refinance your car, so even after you sign on the dotted line, it is not too late. I have refinanced two of my cars. In both cases, I was able to drop the interest on the loan by about 2 percent, which saved me money. Second, the longer you take to repay the loan, the more it will cost you. Paying a little bit extra each month on the loan or making an extra payment or two each year can help reduce the interest you are charged for the car.

- Online bill payment: I have recently become a big fan of online bill payment through my local bank. When a bill arrives, I enter the information on my bank's website, and I am done. It does take a bit of getting used to, but there are advantages, the biggest being that you save time and money (postage) each month. I probably save about $50 a year on postage alone, and because I use the bank's bill payment system, I pay no service charges, including ATM fees, on my bank accounts. While most companies allow you to pay bills on their websites, I feel more in control when I process bills through my bank. I encourage you to check out online bill payment if you have not done so already.

These few suggestions can help you save money here and there. You can search the Internet for many more ideas that fit your lifestyle and buying habits. Not all of the information you find will work for you, but some of it will. Don't feel embarrassed about pinching pennies—after all, many rich people got that way not because they spent money but because they saved it!

For more ways to save, check out the Federal Citizen Information Center's "66 Ways to Save Money" at http://www.pueblo.gsa.gov/cic_text/money/66ways/index.html.

Financial Management Software

Many personal financial software packages are available to consumers. A word of caution: While there are many advantages to using a software package to manage your finances, you must be extremely diligent in using it, entering all of your transactions. Today's programs can be integrated with your bank's online services, which makes the process easier. I tend to leave my personal banking off the computer but use QuickBooks to track my business transactions.

Here are a few things to consider about financial management software programs.

- Check reviews in computer magazines and on the Internet to narrow your choices.
- Compare features and prices of programs.
- Stick with the basic versions of programs unless you want to use a program to monitor investments.
- Compare planning and budgeting features and investment tools if you will use them.
- Find out which program your bank recommends or requires if you wish to integrate with your bank.

- Look for billing, payroll, and invoice features if you need them for business.
- Compare options for exporting your information.
- Compare ease of use.

(eHow.com 2005)

Credit Reports

One thing to do now that you are taking a hard look at your financial situation is to obtain a copy of your credit report. Your credit report includes your current and past addresses, your loan repayment history, and other information, including whether you have been arrested, been sued, or filed for bankruptcy. Businesses use credit reports to verify information and to evaluate their customers and the risks they may represent. Under the Fair Credit Reporting Act (FCRA), nationwide consumer reporting companies must provide you with a free copy of your credit report, at your request, once every twelve months. The easiest way to obtain a copy of your credit report is to visit www.annualcreditreport.com and follow the instructions. This site also has information pertaining to credit repair and fraud.

Debunking the American Dream

We have spent a lot of time talking about how to manage your personal finances. There is still more to learn. But before leaving this important subject, I would like to add one more thing. Like your choice of career, the decisions you make regarding your financial life will be unique and will not quite fit the so-called American dream.

For example, many of the financial books I have read place a lot of value on homeownership. A home is typically the largest asset a person will own, which is great for people for whom owning a home makes sense. For an actor who travels frequently, it makes a bit less sense. Also, people do not talk much about certain aspects of homeownership, the biggest being that a house is not a liquid asset—it can't be quickly converted into cash. And if the owners did sell the house, would they make a lot of money on the sale or not? Sure, looking at the quick equation of sale price minus purchase price, you might think homeownership is a great deal. But add in interest, taxes, yearly upkeep, and maintenance, and it might not look so good.

The point is that you have to really think for yourself about your financial goals in light of your personal and professional goals. There is no one-size-fits-all for financial planning, but the more you know, the better decisions you will be able to make for yourself.

Notes from the Field: Financial Pornography

Financial advisors often refer to the ongoing mass media coverage of the financial markets as financial pornography. It is presented in such a way as to catch your attention and elicit an immediate response, but it has no lasting value.

Advertisers reward media outlets for repeat viewers, so daily financial news outlets are commonly designed to create a sense of urgency that compels you to tune in every day. The message is that if you don't pay attention, you will miss an important financial opportunity that won't be available to you again. Information is presented in short, hurried sound bites that issue a call to action that not so subtly suggests that if you ignore the information, you do so at your own peril.

Unlike a well-written story, where the plot line is so compelling that failing to follow along might truly cause you to miss connecting dialogue, for the long-term investor, financial markets do not require daily attention. "He who hesitates is lost" rarely is true with respect to investing.

—R. F.

Action Items

- Investigate financial management software programs.
- Apply for a copy of your credit report.

9 Your Business Team

As you mature in your career, you will need more and more assistance from people with specific skills: agents, accountants, financial planners, lawyers, and managers. Joining Actors' Equity Association, the union for actors and stage managers, is a good start. Membership in the union includes a fair amount of help with managing your career. Signing with an agent is also a positive development. However, when you enter into a business relationship with an agent, a manager, or anyone else, it is important to have a clear understanding of what is expected of both parties.

The process of finding and signing on to an agency can be an exacerbating experience for a young artist. At first nobody seems to want to talk with you, so when you finally get someone's attention, you jump on the opportunity. But at this critical point in time, you need to step back and ask yourself a few hard questions. Does this person have the skills necessary for what you want to do? What do you want out of this business relationship? Do you feel comfortable with this person? Whether you are signing with an agent or securing the services of a lawyer or tax accountant, there is one extremely important thing to remember: These people are working for you. You pay fees for their services, and these business relationships should be ones of partnership, not dictatorship. You are hiring them as much as they are taking you on as a client, and regardless of what your friends and colleagues may say about them, you need to make sure your relationship is positive and has the ability to meet your expectations. While you must work within the context of a professional relationship, if that relationship is strained or you are unsatisfied, it needs to be terminated. Like all relationships, if communication breaks down, the relationship will falter. Communication is key to all business partnerships such as the one between an actor and his or her agent.

Agents

When it comes to agents, the stories are endless—good and bad. For some, agents are considered the golden ticket to success. After all, they have the ability to get you into auditions that you would not otherwise have access to. You have spent much of your career seeking the attention of agents, so you must be on your way when one of them accepts you as a client. But reality is a bit different than that. The trouble of understanding the role of an agent begins from the start. The journey of most young actors signing on to agencies can be tumultuous if not downright disheartening.

An agent signs an actor because he or she believes that the actor has the potential for a career in the business and that the agent can benefit financially from that success. If you do not work, your agent does not get paid. It is therefore in both of your interests to look for and find you—the actor—a job. An agent's commission is generally set at 10 percent of your earnings, although there are exceptions as outlined in the Actor's Equity Agency Commission Schedule listed below.

> Tier I: No commission on salaries less than the lowest Off Broadway Equity weekly minimum salary (currently $506 per week).

> Tier II: Weekly contractual salaries between the lowest Off-Broadway Equity minimum salary figure (currently $506 per week) and the figure that is the average of the LORT C and LORT D Equity minimum weekly salaries (currently $610.00) shall not be commissionable, except for a service fee of $100. After 10 weeks of public performance, however, a 10% commission shall be applicable. No commission shall be applicable for the rehearsal period.

Tier III: For salaries in excess of the LORT C and LORT D average (currently $610.00), a 10% commission shall be applicable,
except that the rehearsal period at minimum salary shall not
exceed 5% commission." (Actor's Equity Association 2006b)

Even if you are getting work you need to be above the LORT C
and LORT D average for the agent to truly benefit from his or her
work. But, thankfully, the world is not that cynical. Often agents
sign on actors not only with the belief in the potential for success
but also with the understanding that more time may be needed to
get there. In other words, agents are willing to work with you.

In general, it is the role of the agent to represent clients by
sending them to auditions that the agent learned about through the
Breakdown Service, which is available only to franchised agencies
and other trade channels. Having an agent does open more doors of
opportunity, but you still need to walk through those doors and audition along with a lot of other people who also have agents.

If you receive a role, your agent will negotiate your contract
with the producer or the producing organization. Obviously, your
agent has a vested interest in getting the best possible compensation for you; the size of the agent's commission depends on it. In
my experience, as someone who has negotiated contracts with
both agents and the actors themselves, negotiating with agents
was not necessarily unpleasant, but it was more challenging than
negotiating directly with actors. After all, it was my job as a producer to hire the best talent for the lowest possible expense to the
organization. Actors definitely lost out more than a few times by
negotiating their own contracts.

If you do have an agent interested in you, here are a few
things to consider. Before jumping with joy, make sure the agent
is legitimate. All legitimate agents are franchised through at least
one of the three major unions: Actors' Equity Association (AEA),
the Screen Actors Guild (SAG), and the American Federation of
Television and Radio Artists (AFTRA). These unions provide lists
of franchised agents. SAG's website www.sag.org has this information readily available. If the person asking you to come in for an
interview is not franchised, do not bother wasting your time. If he
or she is legitimate, go to the interview well prepared.

At this critical juncture in your career, you must forget about
all that you have had to endure to reach your first interview with

an agent. If you sign with an agent just to have an agent, you may be making a big mistake. This is the beginning of a possible business relationship, and while you want to impress the agent with your experience and talent, you do not want to cloud the fact that the agent should also be selling his or her good points to you. You too have something to offer to the agent.

As Robert Cohen suggests in *Acting Professionally* (1998), you need to ask questions of the agent. Like all good interviews, this should not be a one-sided conversation. You need to know how the agent sees you and whether that agrees with what you think and want. Ask about the agent's plan for using you. How do you fit with his or her other clients? Ultimately, you are trying to get a sense of how enthusiastic the agent is about you and whether they see your career trajectory as you see it (Cohen 1998, p. 109). Whenever you consider hiring professionals, you need to ask questions to determine whether you agree with their thinking and whether they have something to offer you. Actors hire agents for their expertise; if you do not feel sufficiently confident in how an agent will represent you or in his or her ability to find you sufficient work, it is probably best to leave the interview without signing anything. Try again later with an agent you do feel confident in and comfortable with.

Notes from the Field: Good Impressions

A bit of advice on making a good impression with casting directors, agents, directors, employers, or anyone else whom you'd like to impress in a meeting: Ask a lot of questions about them and their experiences. Essentially, count how many times you say "you" and "yours" as opposed to "I," "me," and "mine," and make sure there are more incidences of the former group than of the latter. Sure, you're there so these people can gain information about you and your abilities, but more is to be gleaned from how you interact with and take an active interest in others. When you're able to answer questions succinctly and then volley topics back into their court, people will immediately be impressed by your genuine curiosity and eagerness to learn everything you can about them and/or their projects. I've always gone by the idea that if they've answered more questions about their experiences than they've asked me, it was a successful interview.

—K. S.

Managers

I can never understand the role of a manager for an actor, especially for an actor on the way up. Sure, once you arrive, a quality manager can serve you well, but what is the difference between an agent and a manager? Not much and yet a lot. Managers are not franchised and therefore are not controlled by any of the unions. Typically, a manager charges a 15 percent commission. You pay this in addition to the 10 percent your agent gets since managers cannot negotiate actor contracts. Managers help manage your career as well as assist you with the business of your career. They serve as another person on your team supporting your work and, more importantly, looking for more work. A good and trusting agent will certainly provide you with similar guidance and counsel.

Before signing on with a manager, you need to be clear about the benefits you will gain from this partnership. Perhaps a less exciting relationship with a good lawyer or an accountant would serve you better in the long run.

Notes from the Field: Keeping Professional and Cultivating Contacts

Your professional reputation is much like your credit report—except that instead of it *following* you around, it goes *before* you throughout your career. You must foster and maintain a level of respect with everyone you encounter, in the theatre as well as in life—regardless of how they can or cannot assist you in your goals. These are life rules, not just career rules. People should simply treat other people better! The most challenging times to maintain a sense of professionalism is when things do not work out the way you'd hoped. At these times, as my grandfather used to paraphrase a saying by Mark Twain, you must take the high road, which may be a lonely road, but it's the *only* road.

Take responsibility for your actions. If you are late, admit it and move on. Don't blame the receptionist or the proctor at the audition and say that you were given the wrong location. Bring your best work with you everywhere you audition—and when you still don't get the part, even after three callbacks, take the time to write a heartfelt thank-you note to the producers, director, and casting director (and their assistants) about what an interesting process it was, and how thrilling it was to get so close to being a part of their project, and how you hope you'll have the opportunity to work with them someday.

If someone went out of his or her way for you, acknowledge that in the note. For example, to the administrative assistant in the casting director's office, I would write, "You were always so pleasant with me over the phone, especially when I called in a panic because I'd gone to the wrong location for the audition and you managed to move me to a later slot!" In six months' time, this person could be the casting assistant—but you don't write the note in anticipation of that, but rather because it's the right thing to do to establish a relationship.

To the producer or director, I might write, "What a whirlwind three weeks this has been, since my first audition (an Equity Principal Audition or EPA!) through to the final callback. I look forward to seeing the show and will be proud that I was part of the earliest stages of its development. I hope we'll have the opportunity to work together in the future." A simple note, handwritten, goes a long way because it's personal. It can also serve as closure for you. Learn from your mistakes, and when things outside of your control go awry, take them a little less seriously.

Try to avoid negative thoughts, actions, and people in situations where you are about to show your work. Our own thoughts can be powerful critics and make us lose confidence in ourselves. As our thoughts get more desperate—"I really need this job"—our behavior communicates that as well, and then we push, or rush, or don't listen. Actors often tell me, "I don't audition well," but often it's because they're making it personal rather than professional. A director is like a person trying on clothes at the store—he or she will decide, for whatever reason, which ones to buy, and it's often a matter of fit, which is extremely subjective. Unfortunately, in this metaphor, the clothes are actors, people who have feelings—but the feelings can't contribute to either getting the job or doing your best work.

Sometimes you will encounter important industry people in places outside of their professional capacity, or you may become friends with someone in a position to help your career. These are delicate matters and require a higher level of professionalism. I'm paraphrasing here, but I think it was Ben Cameron, former Executive Director of Theatre Communications Group, who said, jokingly, on moving into philanthropy, "I may never have to pay for lunch again, but I've received my last sincere compliment." No one wants to feel used or to feel that others speak to him or her only as a chance to improve their

continued

own careers. When you encounter an important industry professional at a play, a restaurant, or even the corner grocery store, it's an opportunity to make a connection and establish a relationship without turning it into an audition or handing him or her your screenplay. The secret is to make the encounter about *the other person*, not you.

If you encounter professionals outside a performance, tell the director how much you enjoyed the play he or she recently directed, or ask the casting director how it feels to see the finished product. They are in "theatre mode," and industry-related conversations are appropriate. Always introduce yourself, and if you've met them before, remind them when. For example, if during an intermission I saw an agent I'd been trying to get an appointment with, I'd say, "Hello, I'm Catherine Weidner, with The Shakespeare Theatre Company; we met last year when you came to Washington to see your client Patrick Page as Iago in *Othello*." This way I'd not only introduce myself but also give the agent a first topic for conversation. I'd gauge how the exchange was going, and if it seemed appropriate, I could say, "Patrick speaks so highly of you; I wish I could find representation like that!" If it didn't seem like the right time for a plug, I'd simply say, "What do you think of tonight's performance so far?" or "Do you represent someone in the cast?"

If you see the assistant to someone, never ask whether his or her boss is present. Just be happy to see the assistant, say hello, and keep the conversation about him or her.

If you encounter an industry professional in a nontheatre setting, say, at the grocery store, you should certainly say hello, introduce yourself, say you're a fan of his or her work, and so on, but then keep the conversation light—without making a big plug for yourself. Again, gauge the situation and act accordingly and appropriately: If the person is choosing between two brands of salsa, just say which one you think is a better spicy (or mild) salsa. And if you see this person buying items of a personal nature, it's best to not intrude and to just walk by. You can go home and tell your friend, "You'll never believe who was buying (*insert questionable purchase here*) at the (*insert unlikely location here*)."

If you are friends with someone who is in a position that might better your career, it's important to delineate at the *outset* of a particular contact whether your call or email is personal or professional. If you want to go to the movies or grab coffee on the weekend, use this friend's personal email or home or personal cell phone number, and make no mention of business whatsoever. If it is a business-related matter (and we often do business with our closest friends), use the office and business phones and email only. Get to the point quickly, after checking in briefly, of course—"How are the kids/dogs/and so on?" "How was your vacation? I want to see the pictures!"—and then move on: "I'm calling because I need your help getting an audition for this Broadway show." Nothing feels more awkward than talking to an old friend I haven't seen for fifteen years who calls me at the office, talks for half an hour catching up on our lives, and then asks for help getting an audition. I would rather have such people say, "I'm in town for a couple of days trying to get an audition for this new show, and I was wondering if you wanted to have lunch so we could catch up. I know you're close to the director, so I don't know if you'd feel comfortable asking her to see me, but either way, I'd love to have lunch with you on Saturday." Then they're being straightforward about the favor and genuine about wanting to get together.

The most important things to remember are to gauge what's happening between you and the person you've encountered and to resist the temptation to cross the line into self-promotion. If you have difficulty imagining why someone wouldn't want to hear about your special project, imagine what it would feel like if the tables were turned and everywhere you went people were handing you their headshots, résumés, or screenplays.

There's an old saying: "There are only twenty-five people in the American theatre." This means that everyone knows everyone else, has worked with everyone else, or knows someone else who has. Everything you say has power, so be mindful of your words. Everything you do has an impact, so behave in a way that reflects your best intentions, whether in auditions, rehearsals, backstage, or in the produce aisle. Manners count.

—C. W.

Tax Accountants

Chapter 7 covered the ins and outs of taxes for performing artists. However, sometime your tax situation may become too complex for your attention and patience. This would be a good time to consider hiring a personal tax preparer.

If you are still on the fence and do not want to share more of your hard-earned money, you could use Equity's Volunteer Income

Tax Assistance (VITA) program. "VITA is an IRS-sponsored tax assistance program that was initiated by Equity in the 1970s. It is run on a volunteer basis by IRS-trained members and provides free tax preparation to members of Equity and other performing arts unions. There are currently programs in New York, Los Angeles, Seattle and Orlando" (Actors' Equity Association 2006c). Otherwise, you could go one step further and hire a tax accountant.

Many people think of H&R Block when they think of tax preparers. H&R Block is the most recognizable tax services company in the United States. But because you work in a specialized field that has a unique set of rules regarding tax filings, it might be best to find a tax accountant who deals primarily with artists and entertainment people. These tax preparers are particularly focused on changes in the tax laws that affect their clients—actors like you.

Again, remember that you are the boss of the relationship, and your tax accountant's ability to perform at his or her best requires your attention. When looking for a good tax accountant, begin with the recommendations of your friends and colleagues. However, keep in mind that the size of one's tax refund is not the best indicator of a good tax accountant. People's earnings and tax obligations are different. Instead of comparing tax refunds, it is best to ask questions about the quality of service.

As R. Brendan Hanlon explains in his book *The New Tax Guide for Performers, Writers, Directors, Designers, and Other Show Biz Folk* (1999), good tax preparers are willing to spend time with their clients. They are available to their clients throughout the year to answer questions. If you were to be audited by the IRS, your tax accountant should help you prepare for the audit and represent you at your meeting (Hanlon 1999).

But even if you have someone else prepare your tax filings, you still have to take an active role in the process. You should ask your tax preparer to explain anything you do not understand. If you find exaggerations or inventions on your tax forms, you need to have them done over and done correctly. If that happens, you should also start looking for a new tax accountant. You are responsible for what is contained in these filings, and you will pay any fees or fines that result from exaggerations—it is not worth the risk (Hanlon 1999).

Rates for tax preparation services can vary. Some accountants charge an hourly rate; your bill may vary based on the size and complexity of your filings. Others charge on a sliding scale. This kind of arrangement works well if your earnings fluctuate from year to year. The question to ask: Are you getting what you paid for? Remember that the size of your refund is not the only consideration.

Financial Planners

Just like the rest of your business team, your financial planner should be someone who has an understanding of your financial needs, is willing to work with you, and can help set financial goals for your future. Most people make the mistake of assuming that financial planners are only for wealthy people. But the truth is that a financial planner's job is to help you build wealth over time. As your wealth and assets grow, so too will your planner's fees. In some ways, this is like an agent signing an actor believed to have the potential for a great and prosperous career. You are in essence creating a win-win situation. If a financial planner is interested only in what you can invest today, you are probably in the wrong office.

As when looking for the services of other professionals, a good place to start is with recommendations from friends and colleagues. Ask whether they're happy with the services offered by their advisors. It is a good idea to meet with a few advisors before making a decision. The Certified Financial Planner Board of Standards recommends asking the following questions as a good comparison among planners.

10 Questions to Ask When Choosing a Financial Planner
1. What experience do you have?
2. What are your qualifications?
3. What services do you offer?
4. What is your approach to financial planning?
5. Will you be the only person working with me?
6. How will I pay for your services?
7. How much do you typically charge?
8. Could anyone besides me benefit from your recommendations?
9. Have you ever been publicly disciplined for any unlawful or unethical actions in your professional career?
10. Can I have it in writing?

(Certified Financial Planner Board of Standards 2006)

There are many places to look for financial advisors, banks, investment firms, and individual agencies. Regardless, the person you engage should be certified.

Notes from the Field: What Do I Pay Attention To?

You should pay attention to your own long-term plan. Work with a reputable financial advisor to create a long-term investment strategy that you can follow. Reputable financial advisors will customize a financial plan as a routine step toward creating a wealth-building strategy.

Your success in creating financial stability primarily depends on how much and how often you save money. Financial advisors can help you create a long-term savings program within your means and project the long-term results.

Once a wealth-building strategy has been identified, you should start investing some of your hard-earned income, preferably in a tax-deferred retirement plan that you open for yourself or your employer creates for you. Remember that a retirement plan is a way to save money so that sometime in the future you will not have to work as hard as you do today.

Long-term financial stability is your responsibility. The government and employers have successfully shifted that responsibility to you. The good news is that with a well-defined strategy, implemented early in your work life, you have a very good chance of meeting your goals without sacrificing a satisfying current lifestyle.

Conversely, the longer you wait to save and to implement a strategy, the more restricted your current lifestyle will be. So start saving as soon as you have income.

—R. F.

Action Items

- Ask your friends and colleagues about their professional advisors.
- When you're ready, hire the necessary people to create your team.

onclusion

Corporation You

Envision for me, if you will, that you are the CEO of a midsize corporation. It is morning, and you are preparing to go to work. You are going over your schedule for the day. You are comfortable with your tasks because you know that you will be able to accomplish these goals in the given time restraints of a single day. You also know that these activities align with your overall values and goals.

Your first meeting of the day is with the human resources director. You are briefed on employee training programs, improvements in health policies, and internal efforts to lead the staff to healthier lifestyles and fitness programs. Oddly, the director looks like you. Your next appointment is with the accounting staff. They present you with reports on the financial condition of the organization. The discussion includes strategies for handling temporary cash flow problems as well as long-term investment options. Again the people look a bit like you. Next you meet with the marketing director, who reports on the return rate of a recent direct mail campaign and the follow-up being prepared. You meet with the public relations director, who discusses work on a new blog and a MySpace account. You make a few calls to outside consultants hired to assist in reaching the company's vision.

Finally, you head down to the research and development lab to see how the company's primary product is being enhanced and improved. You stand looking at your prized product—you. This is not a company in the traditional sense. This company is you: Actor, Inc.

The goal of this book is to shatter the traditional paradigm of what it means to be a working actor and to move you to that of an artistic entrepreneur. Many of the books available today that address acting careers go only so far. As an actor, you have to be responsible for your entire career, not just the one on stage. It is possible to stumble through life, but as you have read, it does not have to be that way.

Having Plans, Setting Goals, and Implementing Action

When most people embark on their acting careers, they do not have a solid plan before them. They move to New York City for theatre or to Los Angeles to be in films. But do they even know where their best talents lie? Or are they putting aside major strengths and abilities in one area for a dream of another? Pursuing a career in the arts is not an easy task, but if you enter into it with a clear understanding of the challenges and opportunities ahead, you are less likely to be surprised or caught off guard. You are less likely to get depressed about your career because you anticipated the path would have ups and downs.

The two most valuable resources a person or business has are time and money. Of course, time is connected to money in the sense that we have to give up our time to make money. This is especially poignant for actors because they know there is a huge difference between giving time to earn income as an actor and just working a job to make money.

Managing your time and money is a valuable exercise for anyone running a business. By writing out goals and strategies to reach those goals, you can set priorities. This way, you are not wasting time doing things that do not bring you closer to *your* goals. You will learn to respond properly to outside influences bringing in urgent but not important activities to you. You will grow to be *proactive* rather than *reactive*. By managing your time, you will have the freedom to do the things you want to do, not just the things you have to do. Perhaps you will gain more time just to relax once in a while.

In much the same way, by managing your money in an objective and active manner, you can achieve your financial goals over the long term. While you are not always in control of how much money you earn for the work you perform, you are in control of how you spend it. By keeping your life in financial balance, you can be happy by focusing on your personal financial goals. Money is very personal. In fact, it is one of the main reasons why marriages fail. People spend money in accordance with their own needs and wants. You have to determine your basic needs and wants and then be comfortable with the choices you have made, knowing that this plan works for you. Earning more money is not the only way to become wealthier. Even with a modest income, people can achieve financial independence. They do so by paying attention to their financial health, setting goals for their money, and achieving those goals. We can achieve financial security by keeping our monthly expenses at modest levels, having our money work for us in investment accounts, and taking advantage of tax incentives and credits. I realize that many of you probably have never taken a business course or read through financial publications, but the secret is that it is not rocket science. Once you read a book or two, you will begin to see themes and patterns developing. There are some simple financial rules that if followed will help you improve your financial situation.

As with a business, the people you bring on board to assist you in your work should be qualified as well as committed to your goals. Agents, accountants, managers, and financial planners are all great assets to your future success, but not if they are a poor match. When looking for new people, businesses go through an extensive process to find and select the best person for the job—the candidate who not only has the skills and training to complete the job but also shares values similar to those of the corporation. When you begin to reach out for your own staff, it would behoove you to mimic the corporate process by asking a lot of questions and seeking references for every candidate. It is okay to make mistakes, but it is even better to avoid them altogether.

Each year many new business books are published and sold. Why are these books so popular? Because, like actors reading acting technique books, businesspeople are looking for new ideas to incorporate into their business enterprises. I challenge you now to expand on your yearly reading selections and to include a few books on personal finance and time management. Over time, you will pick up things here and there and implement them into your own strategies. You might be surprised how things from seemingly different points of view come together. I was surprised to find connections between Stephen Covey's *The Seven Habits of Highly Effective People* (1989) and Don Miguel Ruiz's *The Four Agreements* (2001). Similar connections can also be found in many of today's personal finance books. But you must keep at it. Progress is an ongoing process. But when results begin to happen, it will be worth your effort.

I am writing this book at the close of the year. I have recently moved to a new city, and by tracking my expenses for a few months, I was able to get an exact measure of my spending habits and generate strategies on how to reduce my daily expenses. It has served me well. Now, as I do at least once a year, sometimes twice, with my personal mission statement in hand and my goals written out, I am going through my list to see what I have and have not accomplished. My list includes personal, professional, and financial goals. I am always a bit surprised by what I have accomplished, but I never stress over the things I have not done. There is always next year. At the beginning of the year, I recalculate my net worth and make goals on ways to increase that wealth. With all of this in hand, I write out my goals for the year to come. I try very hard to evaluate my life, the roles and responsibilities I have in life as well as my core values and beliefs.

A life in the arts can be a tumultuous existence filled with extreme highs and lows. For me, as I hope for you, it has been well worth the ride. Along the way, I have learned a lot about the art that I love and about how to manage a life in the arts. I sincerely hope that you find the tools contained in this book helpful and that it eases some of the bumps along the way without diminishing the highs you will experience.

Action Item

- Go out there and have a great career and life!

Appendices

Tax Forms

Appendix A

Form 1040 2006 (Page 1)

Form **1040**	Department of the Treasury—Internal Revenue Service **U.S. Individual Income Tax Return**	2006	(99)	IRS Use Only—Do not write or staple in this space.

For the year Jan. 1–Dec. 31, 2006, or other tax year beginning , 2006, ending , 20   OMB No. 1545-0074

Label
(See instructions on page 16.)
Use the IRS label.
Otherwise, please print or type.

LABEL HERE

Your first name and initial	Last name	Your social security number
If a joint return, spouse's first name and initial	Last name	Spouse's social security number

Home address (number and street). If you have a P.O. box, see page 16.   Apt. no.

City, town or post office, state, and ZIP code. If you have a foreign address, see page 16.

▲ You **must** enter your SSN(s) above. ▲

Presidential Election Campaign ▶ Check here if you, or your spouse if filing jointly, want $3 to go to this fund (see page 16) ▶ ☐ You ☐ Spouse

Checking a box below will not change your tax or refund.

Filing Status
Check only one box.

1 ☐ Single
2 ☐ Married filing jointly (even if only one had income)
3 ☐ Married filing separately. Enter spouse's SSN above and full name here. ▶
4 ☐ Head of household (with qualifying person). (See page 17.) If the qualifying person is a child but not your dependent, enter this child's name here. ▶
5 ☐ Qualifying widow(er) with dependent child (see page 17)

Exemptions

6a ☐ **Yourself.** If someone can claim you as a dependent, **do not** check box 6a
b ☐ **Spouse** . . . .

c **Dependents:**

(1) First name Last name	(2) Dependent's social security number	(3) Dependent's relationship to you	(4) ✓ if qualifying child for child tax credit (see page 19)
			☐
			☐
			☐
			☐

If more than four dependents, see page 19.

d Total number of exemptions claimed . . . .

Boxes checked on 6a and 6b ___
No. of children on 6c who:
• lived with you ___
• did not live with you due to divorce or separation (see page 20) ___
Dependents on 6c not entered above ___
Add numbers on lines above ▶ ☐

Income

Attach Form(s) W-2 here. Also attach Forms W-2G and 1099-R if tax was withheld.

If you did not get a W-2, see page 23.

Enclose, but do not attach, any payment. Also, please use Form 1040-V.

7	Wages, salaries, tips, etc. Attach Form(s) W-2	7	
8a	**Taxable** interest. Attach Schedule B if required	8a	
b	Tax-exempt interest. **Do not** include on line 8a . . .	8b	
9a	Ordinary dividends. Attach Schedule B if required	9a	
b	Qualified dividends (see page 23)	9b	
10	Taxable refunds, credits, or offsets of state and local income taxes (see page 24)	10	
11	Alimony received	11	
12	Business income or (loss). Attach Schedule C or C-EZ	12	
13	Capital gain or (loss). Attach Schedule D if required. If not required, check here ▶ ☐	13	
14	Other gains or (losses). Attach Form 4797	14	
15a	IRA distributions . 15a	b Taxable amount (see page 25)	15b	
16a	Pensions and annuities 16a	b Taxable amount (see page 26)	16b	
17	Rental real estate, royalties, partnerships, S corporations, trusts, etc. Attach Schedule E	17	
18	Farm income or (loss). Attach Schedule F	18	
19	Unemployment compensation	19	
20a	Social security benefits . 20a	b Taxable amount (see page 27)	20b	
21	Other income. List type and amount (see page 29)	21	
22	Add the amounts in the far right column for lines 7 through 21. This is your **total income** ▶	22	

Adjusted Gross Income

23	Archer MSA deduction. Attach Form 8853 .	23	
24	Certain business expenses of reservists, performing artists, and fee-basis government officials. Attach Form 2106 or 2106-EZ	24	
25	Health savings account deduction. Attach Form 8889 . .	25	
26	Moving expenses. Attach Form 3903	26	
27	One-half of self-employment tax. Attach Schedule SE . .	27	
28	Self-employed SEP, SIMPLE, and qualified plans .	28	
29	Self-employed health insurance deduction (see page 29)	29	
30	Penalty on early withdrawal of savings	30	
31a	Alimony paid b Recipient's SSN ▶	31a	
32	IRA deduction (see page 31)	32	
33	Student loan interest deduction (see page 33) . . .	33	
34	Jury duty pay you gave to your employer . . .	34	
35	Domestic production activities deduction. Attach Form 8903	35	
36	Add lines 23 through 31a and 32 through 35 . . . . ▶	36	
37	Subtract line 36 from line 22. This is your **adjusted gross income** . . . . . . ▶	37	

For Disclosure, Privacy Act, and Paperwork Reduction Act Notice, see page 80.   Cat. No. 11320B   Form **1040** (2006)

Appendix A
Form 1040 2006 (Page 2)

Tax and Credits	38	Amount from line 37 (adjusted gross income)	38
	39a	Check { ☐ **You** were born before January 2, 1942, ☐ Blind. } **Total boxes**	
		if: { ☐ **Spouse** was born before January 2, 1942, ☐ Blind. } checked ▶ 39a	
Standard Deduction for—	b	If your spouse itemizes on a separate return or you were a dual-status alien, see page 34 and check here ▶39b ☐	
	40	**Itemized deductions** (from Schedule A) **or** your **standard deduction** (see left margin) . .	40
• People who checked any box on line 39a or 39b **or** who can be claimed as a dependent, see page 34.	41	Subtract line 40 from line 38	41
	42	If line 38 is over $112,875, or you provided housing to a person displaced by Hurricane Katrina, see page 36. Otherwise, multiply $3,300 by the total number of exemptions claimed on line 6d	42
	43	**Taxable income.** Subtract line 42 from line 41. If line 42 is more than line 41, enter -0- .	43
	44	**Tax** (see page 36). Check if any tax is from: **a** ☐ Form(s) 8814 **b** ☐ Form 4972 . . .	44
• All others:	45	**Alternative minimum tax** (see page 39). Attach Form 6251	45
Single or Married filing separately, $5,150	46	Add lines 44 and 45 . . . . ▶	46
	47	Foreign tax credit. Attach Form 1116 if required	47	
	48	Credit for child and dependent care expenses. Attach Form 2441	48	
	49	Credit for the elderly or the disabled. Attach Schedule R .	49	
Married filing jointly or Qualifying widow(er), $10,300	50	Education credits. Attach Form 8863	50	
	51	Retirement savings contributions credit. Attach Form 8880 . .	51	
	52	Residential energy credits. Attach Form 5695	52	
Head of household, $7,550	53	Child tax credit (see page 42). Attach Form 8901 if required	53	
	54	Credits from: **a** ☐ Form 8396 **b** ☐ Form 8839 **c** ☐ Form 8859	54	
	55	Other credits: **a** ☐ Form 3800 **b** ☐ Form 8801 **c** ☐ Form___	55	
	56	Add lines 47 through 55. These are your **total credits**	56
	57	Subtract line 56 from line 46. If line 56 is more than line 46, enter -0- . . . . . ▶	57
Other Taxes	58	Self-employment tax. Attach Schedule SE	58
	59	Social security and Medicare tax on tip income not reported to employer. Attach Form 4137 . .	59
	60	Additional tax on IRAs, other qualified retirement plans, etc. Attach Form 5329 if required . .	60
	61	Advance earned income credit payments from Form(s) W-2, box 9	61
	62	Household employment taxes. Attach Schedule H	62
	63	Add lines 57 through 62. This is your **total tax** . . . . ▶	63
Payments	64	Federal income tax withheld from Forms W-2 and 1099 . .	64	
	65	2006 estimated tax payments and amount applied from 2005 return	65	
If you have a qualifying child, attach Schedule EIC.	66a	**Earned income credit (EIC)**	66a	
	b	Nontaxable combat pay election ▶	66b	
	67	Excess social security and tier 1 RRTA tax withheld (see page 60)	67	
	68	Additional child tax credit. Attach Form 8812	68	
	69	Amount paid with request for extension to file (see page 60)	69	
	70	Payments from: **a** ☐ Form 2439 **b** ☐ Form 4136 **c** ☐ Form 8885	70	
	71	Credit for federal telephone excise tax paid. Attach Form 8913 if required	71	
	72	Add lines 64, 65, 66a, and 67 through 71. These are your **total payments** . . . . ▶	72
Refund	73	If line 72 is more than line 63, subtract line 63 from line 72. This is the amount you **overpaid**	73
Direct deposit? See page 61 and fill in 74b, 74c, and 74d, or Form 8888.	74a	Amount of line 73 you want **refunded to you.** If Form 8888 is attached, check here ▶ ☐	74a
	▶ b	Routing number [ ][ ][ ][ ][ ][ ][ ][ ][ ] ▶ c Type: ☐ Checking ☐ Savings	
	▶ d	Account number [ ][ ][ ][ ][ ][ ][ ][ ][ ][ ][ ][ ][ ][ ][ ][ ][ ]	
	75	Amount of line 73 you want **applied to your 2007 estimated tax** ▶	75	
Amount You Owe	76	**Amount you owe.** Subtract line 72 from line 63. For details on how to pay, see page 62 ▶	76
	77	Estimated tax penalty (see page 62)	77	

Third Party Designee	Do you want to allow another person to discuss this return with the IRS (see page 63)? ☐ **Yes.** Complete the following. ☐ **No**
	Designee's name ▶ Phone no. ▶ ( ) Personal identification number (PIN) ▶ [ ][ ][ ][ ][ ]

Sign Here
Joint return? See page 17.
Keep a copy for your records.

Under penalties of perjury, I declare that I have examined this return and accompanying schedules and statements, and to the best of my knowledge and belief, they are true, correct, and complete. Declaration of preparer (other than taxpayer) is based on all information of which preparer has any knowledge.

Your signature	Date	Your occupation	Daytime phone number ( )
Spouse's signature. If a joint return, **both** must sign.	Date	Spouse's occupation	

Paid Preparer's Use Only

Preparer's signature ▶	Date	Check if self-employed ☐	Preparer's SSN or PTIN
Firm's name (or yours if self-employed), address, and ZIP code ▶		EIN	
		Phone no. ( )	

Appendix B
Schedules A & B (Page 1)

SCHEDULES A&B	Schedule A—Itemized Deductions	OMB No. 1545-0074
(Form 1040)	(Schedule B is on back)	2006
Department of the Treasury Internal Revenue Service (99)	▶ Attach to Form 1040. ▶ See Instructions for Schedules A&B (Form 1040).	Attachment Sequence No. 07
Name(s) shown on Form 1040		Your social security number

Medical		**Caution.** Do not include expenses reimbursed or paid by others.		
and	1	Medical and dental expenses (see page A-1) . . .	1	
Dental	2	Enter amount from Form 1040, line 38 ⌐ 2 ⌐		
Expenses	3	Multiply line 2 by 7.5% (.075).	3	
	4	Subtract line 3 from line 1. If line 3 is more than line 1, enter -0-.		4
Taxes You	5	State and local income taxes	5	
Paid	6	Real estate taxes (see page A-3)	6	
(See	7	Personal property taxes	7	
page A-3.)	8	Other taxes. List type and amount ▶		
			8	
	9	Add lines 5 through 8		9
Interest	10	Home mortgage interest and points reported to you on Form 1098	10	
You Paid	11	Home mortgage interest not reported to you on Form 1098. If paid		
(See		to the person from whom you bought the home, see page A-3		
page A-3.)		and show that person's name, identifying no., and address ▶		
		. . . .		
Note.		. . . .	11	
Personal interest is	12	Points not reported to you on Form 1098. See page A-4		
not		for special rules	12	
deductible.	13	Investment interest. Attach Form 4952 if required. (See		
		page A-4.)	13	
	14	Add lines 10 through 13		14
Gifts to	15	Gifts by cash or check. If you made any gift of $250 or		
Charity		more, see page A-5	15	
If you made a	16	Other than by cash or check. If any gift of $250 or more,		
gift and got a		see page A-5. You **must** attach Form 8283 if over $500	16	
benefit for it,	17	Carryover from prior year	17	
see page A-4.	18	Add lines 15 through 17		18
Casualty and				
Theft Losses	19	Casualty or theft loss(es). Attach Form 4684. (See page A-6.)		19
Job Expenses	20	Unreimbursed employee expenses—job travel, union		
and Certain		dues, job education, etc. Attach Form 2106 or 2106-EZ		
Miscellaneous		if required. (See page A-6.) ▶	20	
Deductions	21	Tax preparation fees.	21	
(See	22	Other expenses—investment, safe deposit box, etc. List		
page A-6.)		type and amount ▶		
			22	
	23	Add lines 20 through 22	23	
	24	Enter amount from Form 1040, line 38 ⌐ 24 ⌐		
	25	Multiply line 24 by 2% (.02)	25	
	26	Subtract line 25 from line 23. If line 25 is more than line 23, enter -0-		26
Other	27	Other—from list on page A-7. List type and amount ▶		
Miscellaneous		. . . .		
Deductions				27
Total	28	Is Form 1040, line 38, over $150,500 (over $75,250 if married filing separately)?		
Itemized		☐ **No.** Your deduction is not limited. Add the amounts in the far right column		
Deductions		for lines 4 through 27. Also, enter this amount on Form 1040, line 40. ⎫		28
		☐ **Yes.** Your deduction may be limited. See page A-7 for the amount to enter. ⎭		
	29	If you elect to itemize deductions even though they are less than your standard deduction, check here ▶ ☐		

For Paperwork Reduction Act Notice, see Form 1040 instructions.   Cat. No. 11330X   Schedule A (Form 1040) 2006

Appendix B
Schedules A & B (Page 2)

OMB No. 1545-0074   Page **2**

Name(s) shown on Form 1040. Do not enter name and social security number if shown on other side. | Your social security number

Schedule B—Interest and Ordinary Dividends

Attachment Sequence No. **08**

		Amount

Part I Interest

(See page B-1 and the instructions for Form 1040, line 8a.)

Note. If you received a Form 1099-INT, Form 1099-OID, or substitute statement from a brokerage firm, list the firm's name as the payer and enter the total interest shown on that form.

1 List name of payer. If any interest is from a seller-financed mortgage and the buyer used the property as a personal residence, see page B-1 and list this interest first. Also, show that buyer's social security number and address ▶

1

2 Add the amounts on line 1 . . . .   **2**

3 Excludable interest on series EE and I U.S. savings bonds issued after 1989. Attach Form 8815 . . . .   **3**

4 Subtract line 3 from line 2. Enter the result here and on Form 1040, line 8a ▶   **4**

Note. If line 4 is over $1,500, you must complete Part III.

	Amount

Part II Ordinary Dividends

(See page B-1 and the instructions for Form 1040, line 9a.)

Note. If you received a Form 1099-DIV or substitute statement from a brokerage firm, list the firm's name as the payer and enter the ordinary dividends shown on that form.

5 List name of payer ▶

5

6 Add the amounts on line 5. Enter the total here and on Form 1040, line 9a ▶   **6**

Note. If line 6 is over $1,500, you must complete Part III.

Part III Foreign Accounts and Trusts

(See page B-2.)

You must complete this part if you **(a)** had over $1,500 of taxable interest or ordinary dividends; or **(b)** had a foreign account; or **(c)** received a distribution from, or were a grantor of, or a transferor to, a foreign trust.

	Yes	No

7a At any time during 2006, did you have an interest in or a signature or other authority over a financial account in a foreign country, such as a bank account, securities account, or other financial account? See page B-2 for exceptions and filing requirements for Form TD F 90-22.1. . . . . .

b If "Yes," enter the name of the foreign country ▶

8 During 2006, did you receive a distribution from, or were you the grantor of, or transferor to, a foreign trust? If "Yes," you may have to file Form 3520. See page B-2 . . . .

For Paperwork Reduction Act Notice, see Form 1040 instructions.   Schedule B (Form 1040) 2006

Appendix C

Schedule C (Page 1)

SCHEDULE C (Form 1040)	**Profit or Loss From Business**	OMB No. 1545-0074
Department of the Treasury Internal Revenue Service (99)	(Sole Proprietorship) ▶ Partnerships, joint ventures, etc., must file Form 1065 or 1065-B. ▶ Attach to Form 1040, 1040NR, or 1041. ▶ See Instructions for Schedule C (Form 1040).	2006 Attachment Sequence No. 09

Name of proprietor	Social security number (SSN)

A	Principal business or profession, including product or service (see page C-2 of the instructions)	B Enter code from pages C-8, 9, & 10 ▶

C	Business name. If no separate business name, leave blank.	D Employer ID number (EIN), if any

E Business address (including suite or room no.) ▶ ....
City, town or post office, state, and ZIP code

F Accounting method: (1) ☐ Cash (2) ☐ Accrual (3) ☐ Other (specify) ▶ ....
G Did you "materially participate" in the operation of this business during 2006? If "No," see page C-3 for limit on losses   ☐ Yes ☐ No
H If you started or acquired this business during 2006, check here   .   .   .   .   ▶ ☐

Part I Income

1	Gross receipts or sales. **Caution.** If this income was reported to you on Form W-2 and the "Statutory employee" box on that form was checked, see page C-3 and check here . . . . . ▶ ☐	1
2	Returns and allowances	2
3	Subtract line 2 from line 1	3
4	Cost of goods sold (from line 42 on page 2)	4
5	**Gross profit.** Subtract line 4 from line 3.	5
6	Other income, including federal and state gasoline or fuel tax credit or refund (see page C-3). . .	6
7	**Gross income.** Add lines 5 and 6 . . . . ▶	7

Part II Expenses. Enter expenses for business use of your home **only** on line 30.

8	Advertising	8	18	Office expense	18
9	Car and truck expenses (see page C-4).	9	19	Pension and profit-sharing plans	19
10	Commissions and fees . .	10	20	Rent or lease (see page C-5):	
11	Contract labor (see page C-4)	11	a	Vehicles, machinery, and equipment .	20a
12	Depletion	12	b	Other business property . .	20b
13	Depreciation and section 179 expense deduction (not included in Part III) (see page C-4)	13	21	Repairs and maintenance . .	21
			22	Supplies (not included in Part III) .	22
			23	Taxes and licenses . . .	23
			24	Travel, meals, and entertainment:	
14	Employee benefit programs (other than on line 19). .	14	a	Travel	24a
15	Insurance (other than health) .	15	b	Deductible meals and entertainment (see page C-6)	24b
16	Interest:		25	Utilities	25
a	Mortgage (paid to banks, etc.) .	16a	26	Wages (less employment credits)	26
b	Other	16b	27	Other expenses (from line 48 on page 2)	27
17	Legal and professional services	17			

28	**Total expenses** before expenses for business use of home. Add lines 8 through 27 in columns . ▶	28
29	Tentative profit (loss). Subtract line 28 from line 7	29
30	Expenses for business use of your home. Attach **Form 8829**	30
31	**Net profit or (loss).** Subtract line 30 from line 29.	
	• If a profit, enter on both **Form 1040, line 12,** and **Schedule SE, line 2,** or on **Form 1040NR, line 13** (statutory employees, see page C-6). Estates and trusts, enter on Form 1041, line 3.	31
	• If a loss, you **must** go to line 32.	

32 If you have a loss, check the box that describes your investment in this activity (see page C-6).
• If you checked 32a, enter the loss on both **Form 1040, line 12,** and **Schedule SE, line 2,** or on **Form 1040NR, line 13** (statutory employees, see page C-6). Estates and trusts, enter on Form 1041, line 3.
• If you checked 32b, you **must** attach **Form 6198.** Your loss may be limited.

32a ☐ All investment is at risk.
32b ☐ Some investment is not at risk.

For Paperwork Reduction Act Notice, see page C-8 of the instructions.	Cat. No. 11334P	Schedule C (Form 1040) 2006

Appendix C
Schedule C (Page 2)

Part III   **Cost of Goods Sold** (see page C-7)

33   Method(s) used to
value closing inventory: **a** ☐ Cost   **b** ☐ Lower of cost or market   **c** ☐ Other (attach explanation)

34   Was there any change in determining quantities, costs, or valuations between opening and closing inventory?
If "Yes," attach explanation . . . .   ☐ Yes   ☐ No

35 Inventory at beginning of year. If different from last year's closing inventory, attach explanation . .	35	
36 Purchases less cost of items withdrawn for personal use	36	
37 Cost of labor. Do not include any amounts paid to yourself	37	
38 Materials and supplies	38	
39 Other costs	39	
40 Add lines 35 through 39	40	
41 Inventory at end of year	41	
42 **Cost of goods sold.** Subtract line 41 from line 40. Enter the result here and on page 1, line 4 . .	42	

Part IV   **Information on Your Vehicle.** Complete this part **only** if you are claiming car or truck expenses on line 9 and are not required to file Form 4562 for this business. See the instructions for line 13 on page C-4 to find out if you must file Form 4562.

43   When did you place your vehicle in service for business purposes? (month, day, year) ▶ . . . . / . . . . / . . . . . .

44   Of the total number of miles you drove your vehicle during 2006, enter the number of miles you used your vehicle for:

a Business . . . . **b** Commuting (see instructions) . . . . **c** Other . . . .

45   Do you (or your spouse) have another vehicle available for personal use? . . . .   ☐ Yes   ☐ No

46   Was your vehicle available for personal use during off-duty hours? . . . .   ☐ Yes   ☐ No

47a   Do you have evidence to support your deduction? . . . .   ☐ Yes   ☐ No

b   If "Yes," is the evidence written? . . . .   ☐ Yes   ☐ No

Part V   **Other Expenses.** List below business expenses not included on lines 8–26 or line 30.

48 **Total other expenses.** Enter here and on page 1, line 27	48	

Appendix D
Form W-4 2007 (Page 1)

Form W-4 (2007)

Purpose. Complete Form W-4 so that your employer can withhold the correct federal income tax from your pay. Because your tax situation may change, you may want to refigure your withholding each year.

Exemption from withholding. If you are exempt, complete **only** lines 1, 2, 3, 4, and 7 and sign the form to validate it. Your exemption for 2007 expires February 16, 2008. See Pub. 505, Tax Withholding and Estimated Tax.

Note. You cannot claim exemption from withholding if (a) your income exceeds $850 and includes more than $300 of unearned income (for example, interest and dividends) and (b) another person can claim you as a dependent on their tax return.

Basic instructions. If you are not exempt, complete the **Personal Allowances Worksheet** below. The worksheets on page 2 adjust your withholding allowances based on

itemized deductions, certain credits, adjustments to income, or two-earner/multiple job situations. Complete all worksheets that apply. However, you may claim fewer (or zero) allowances.

Head of household. Generally, you may claim head of household filing status on your tax return only if you are unmarried and pay more than 50% of the costs of keeping up a home for yourself and your dependent(s) or other qualifying individuals.

Tax credits. You can take projected tax credits into account in figuring your allowable number of withholding allowances. Credits for child or dependent care expenses and the child tax credit may be claimed using the **Personal Allowances Worksheet** below. See Pub. 919, How Do I Adjust My Tax Withholding, for information on converting your other credits into withholding allowances.

Nonwage income. If you have a large amount of nonwage income, such as interest or dividends, consider making estimated tax payments using Form 1040-ES, Estimated Tax

for Individuals. Otherwise, you may owe additional tax. If you have pension or annuity income, see Pub. 919 to find out if you should adjust your withholding on Form W-4 or W-4P.

Two earners/Multiple jobs. If you have a working spouse or more than one job, figure the total number of allowances you are entitled to claim on all jobs using worksheets from only one Form W-4. Your withholding usually will be most accurate when all allowances are claimed on the Form W-4 for the highest paying job and zero allowances are claimed on the others.

Nonresident alien. If you are a nonresident alien, see the Instructions for Form 8233 before completing this Form W-4.

Check your withholding. After your Form W-4 takes effect, use Pub. 919 to see how the dollar amount you are having withheld compares to your projected total tax for 2007. See Pub. 919, especially if your earnings exceed $130,000 (Single) or $180,000 (Married).

Personal Allowances Worksheet (Keep for your records.)

A   Enter "1" for **yourself** if no one else can claim you as a dependent . . . .   **A** _____

B   Enter "1" if: {
- You are single and have only one job; or
- You are married, have only one job, and your spouse does not work; or
- Your wages from a second job or your spouse's wages (or the total of both) are $1,000 or less.
} . . **B** _____

C   Enter "1" for your **spouse**. But, you may choose to enter "-0-" if you are married and have either a working spouse or more than one job. (Entering "-0-" may help you avoid having too little tax withheld.) . . . . . .   **C** _____

D   Enter number of **dependents** (other than your spouse or yourself) you will claim on your tax return . . . . .   **D** _____

E   Enter "1" if you will file as **head of household** on your tax return (see conditions under **Head of household** above) .   **E** _____

F   Enter "1" if you have at least $1,500 of **child or dependent care expenses** for which you plan to claim a credit . .   **F** _____
(**Note.** Do **not** include child support payments. See Pub. 503, Child and Dependent Care Expenses, for details.)

G   **Child Tax Credit** (including additional child tax credit). See Pub 972, Child Tax Credit, for more information.
- If your total income will be less than $57,000 ($85,000 if married), enter "2" for each eligible child.
- If your total income will be between $57,000 and $84,000 ($85,000 and $119,000 if married), enter "1" for each eligible child plus "1" **additional** if you have 4 or more eligible children. . . . .   **G** _____

H   Add lines A through G and enter total here. (**Note.** This may be different from the number of exemptions you claim on your tax return.) ▶   **H** _____

For accuracy, complete all worksheets that apply. {
- If you plan to **itemize or claim adjustments to income** and want to reduce your withholding, see the **Deductions and Adjustments Worksheet** on page 2.
- If you have **more than one job** or are **married and you and your spouse both work** and the combined earnings from all jobs exceed $40,000 ($25,000 if married) see the **Two-Earners/Multiple Jobs Worksheet** on page 2 to avoid having too little tax withheld.
- If **neither** of the above situations applies, **stop here** and enter the number from line H on line 5 of Form W-4 below.
}

--------------------- Cut here and give Form W-4 to your employer. Keep the top part for your records. ---------------------

Form **W-4**	**Employee's Withholding Allowance Certificate**	OMB No. 1545-0074
Department of the Treasury Internal Revenue Service	▶ Whether you are entitled to claim a certain number of allowances or exemption from withholding is subject to review by the IRS. Your employer may be required to send a copy of this form to the IRS.	2⓪07

1 Type or print your first name and middle initial. Last name	2 Your social security number
Home address (number and street or rural route)	3 ☐ Single ☐ Married ☐ Married, but withhold at higher Single rate. **Note.** If married, but legally separated, or spouse is a nonresident alien, check the "Single" box.
City or town, state, and ZIP code	4 If your last name differs from that shown on your social security card, check here. You must call 1-800-772-1213 for a replacement card. ▶ ☐

5   Total number of allowances you are claiming (from line **H** above **or** from the applicable worksheet on page 2)   **5** _____

6   Additional amount, if any, you want withheld from each paycheck . . . .   **6** $ _____

7   I claim exemption from withholding for 2007, and I certify that I meet **both** of the following conditions for exemption.
- Last year I had a right to a refund of **all** federal income tax withheld because I had **no** tax liability **and**
- This year I expect a refund of **all** federal income tax withheld because I expect to have **no** tax liability.

If you meet both conditions, write "Exempt" here . . . . ▶   **7** _____

Under penalties of perjury, I declare that I have examined this certificate and to the best of my knowledge and belief, it is true, correct, and complete.
Employee's signature
(Form is not valid
unless you sign it.) ▶   **Date** ▶

8 Employer's name and address (Employer: Complete lines 8 and 10 only if sending to the IRS.)	9 Office code (optional)	10 Employer identification number (EIN)

For Privacy Act and Paperwork Reduction Act Notice, see page 2.   Cat. No. 10220Q   Form **W-4** (2007)

128

Appendix D
Form W-4 2007 (Page 2)

Deductions and Adjustments Worksheet

Note. Use this worksheet *only* if you plan to itemize deductions, claim certain credits, or claim adjustments to income on your 2007 tax return.

1	Enter an estimate of your 2007 itemized deductions. These include qualifying home mortgage interest, charitable contributions, state and local taxes, medical expenses in excess of 7.5% of your income, and miscellaneous deductions. (For 2007, you may have to reduce your itemized deductions if your income is over $156,400 ($78,200 if married filing separately). See *Worksheet 2* in Pub. 919 for details.)	1	$
2	Enter: { $10,700 if married filing jointly or qualifying widow(er) / $ 7,850 if head of household / $ 5,350 if single or married filing separately }	2	$
3	**Subtract** line 2 from line 1. If zero or less, enter "-0-"	3	$
4	Enter an estimate of your 2007 adjustments to income, including alimony, deductible IRA contributions, and student loan interest	4	$
5	**Add** lines 3 and 4 and enter the total. (Include any amount for credits from *Worksheet 8* in Pub. 919)	5	$
6	Enter an estimate of your 2007 nonwage income (such as dividends or interest)	6	$
7	**Subtract** line 6 from line 5. If zero or less, enter "-0-"	7	$
8	**Divide** the amount on line 7 by $3,400 and enter the result here. Drop any fraction	8	
9	Enter the number from the **Personal Allowances Worksheet,** line H, page 1	9	
10	**Add** lines 8 and 9 and enter the total here. If you plan to use the **Two-Earners/Multiple Jobs Worksheet,** also enter this total on line 1 below. Otherwise, **stop here** and enter this total on Form W-4, line 5, page 1	10	

Two-Earners/Multiple Jobs Worksheet (See *Two earners/multiple jobs* on page 1.)

Note. Use this worksheet *only* if the instructions under line H on page 1 direct you here.

1	Enter the number from line H, page 1 (or from line 10 above if you used the **Deductions and Adjustments Worksheet**)	1	
2	Find the number in **Table 1** below that applies to the **LOWEST** paying job and enter it here. **However,** if you are married filing jointly and wages from the highest paying job are $50,000 or less, do not enter more than "3."	2	
3	If line 1 is **more than or equal to** line 2, subtract line 2 from line 1. Enter the result here (if zero, enter "-0-") and on Form W-4, line 5, page 1. **Do not** use the rest of this worksheet	3	
Note.	If line 1 is *less than* line 2, enter "-0-" on Form W-4, line 5, page 1. Complete lines 4–9 below to calculate the additional withholding amount necessary to avoid a year-end tax bill.		
4	Enter the number from line 2 of this worksheet	4	
5	Enter the number from line 1 of this worksheet	5	
6	**Subtract** line 5 from line 4	6	
7	Find the amount in **Table 2** below that applies to the **HIGHEST** paying job and enter it here	7	$
8	**Multiply** line 7 by line 6 and enter the result here. This is the additional annual withholding needed	8	$
9	Divide line 8 by the number of pay periods remaining in 2007. For example, divide by 26 if you are paid every two weeks and you complete this form in December 2006. Enter the result here and on Form W-4, line 6, page 1. This is the additional amount to be withheld from each paycheck	9	$

Table 1

Married Filing Jointly		All Others	
If wages from **LOWEST** paying job are—	Enter on line 2 above	If wages from **LOWEST** paying job are—	Enter on line 2 above
$0 - $4,500	0	$0 - $6,000	0
4,501 - 9,000	1	6,001 - 12,000	1
9,001 - 18,000	2	12,001 - 19,000	2
18,001 - 22,000	3	19,001 - 26,000	3
22,001 - 26,000	4	26,001 - 35,000	4
26,001 - 32,000	5	35,001 - 50,000	5
32,001 - 38,000	6	50,001 - 65,000	6
38,001 - 46,000	7	65,001 - 80,000	7
46,001 - 55,000	8	80,001 - 90,000	8
55,001 - 60,000	9	90,001 - 120,000	9
60,001 - 65,000	10	120,001 and over	10
65,001 - 75,000	11		
75,001 - 95,000	12		
95,001 - 105,000	13		
105,001 - 120,000	14		
120,001 and over	15		

Table 2

Married Filing Jointly		All Others	
If wages from **HIGHEST** paying job are—	Enter on line 7 above	If wages from **HIGHEST** paying job are—	Enter on line 7 above
$0 - $65,000	$510	$0 - $35,000	$510
65,001 - 120,000	850	35,001 - 80,000	850
120,001 - 170,000	950	80,001 - 150,000	950
170,001 - 300,000	1,120	150,001 - 340,000	1,120
300,001 and over	1,190	340,001 and over	1,190

Bibliography and Other Suggested Reading

AARON, SUSAN. 2005 "Unemployment Insurance and You." http://content.salary.monster.com/articles/unemployment/. Accessed January 5, 2007.

ACTORS' EQUITY ASSOCIATION. 2006a. "About Equity Handbook." www.actorsequity.org/docs/about/aboutequity_booklet_06.pdf. Accessed May 22, 2007.

———. 2006b. "Agency Commission Schedule." http://www.actorsequity.org/docs/agency/agency_commission.pdf. Accessed June 6, 2007.

———. 2006c. "Volunteer Income Tax Assistance." www.actorsequity.org/Benefits/vita.asp. Accessed September 26, 2006.

ALTERMAN, GLEN. 1998. *Promoting Your Acting Career: A Step-by-Step Guide to Opening the Right Doors*. New York: Allworth Press.

BACH, DAVID. 2003. *The Automatic Millionaire: A Powerful One-Step Plan to Live and Finish Rich*. New York: Broadway.

CARROLL, LEWIS. 1980. *Alice's Adventures in Wonderland*. Franklin Center, PA: The Franklin Library.

CERTIFIED FINANCIAL PLANNER BOARD OF STANDARDS. 2006. "How to Choose a Planner." www.cfp.net/learn/knowledgebase.asp?id=6. Accessed October 16, 2006.

CLEMENTS, JONATHAN. 2006a. "Amid Losses, 12 Financial Truths Persist." *The Wall Street Journal*, June 18, p. 3.

———. 2006b. "Don't Blame the Latte: The Real Reason You're Not Saving More Is Closer to Home." *The Wall Street Journal*, June 21, p. D1.

Cohen, Robert. 1998. *Acting Professionally: Raw Facts About Careers in Acting*. Mountain View, CA Mayfield Publishing.

Covey, Stephen. 1989. *The Seven Habits of Highly Effective People*. New York: Simon & Schuster.

Dominguez, Joe, and Robin, Vicki. 1992. *Your Money or Your Life: Transforming Your Relationship with Money and Achieving Financial Independence*. New York: Viking Press.

Drucker, Peter. 2005. "Managing Oneself." *Harvard Business Review*. Vol. 83 Issue 1, 100–07.

eHow.com. 2005. "How to Choose Personal Financial Management Software." www.ehow.com/how_12634_choose-personal-financial.html. Accessed December 20, 2006.

Grady, Jamie. 2006. *A Simple Statement: A Guide to Arts Management and Leadership*, Portsmouth NH, Heinemann.

Hanlon, R. Brendan. 1999. *The New Tax Guide for Performers, Writers, Directors, Designers, and Other Show Biz Folk*. New York: Limelight Editions.

Internal Revenue Service. 2005a "Publication 529." www.irs.gov/pub/irs-pdf/p529.pdf. Accessed February 16, 2006.

———. 2005b. "Topic 455-Moving Expenses." www.irs.gov/taxtopics/tc455.html. Accessed February 2, 2006.

Kelley, Rob. 2005. "Debt: Consumers Juggle Big Burden." http://money.cnn.com/2005/10/07/pf/debt/debtmeasures/index.htm. Accessed December 20, 2006.

Northwestern Mutual Foundation. 2005. "Places to Invest." www.themint.org/investing/. Accessed December 20, 2006.

O'Neil, Brian. 1999. *Acting as a Business: Strategies for Success*. Portsmouth, NH: Heinemann.

Opdyke, Jeff. 2006. "Will You Be Able to Retire?" *The Wall Street Journal*, July 1–2, p. B1.

RILEY, PETER J. 2002. *The New Tax Guide for Artists of Every Persuasion: Actors, Directors, Musicians, Singers, and Other Show Biz Folk: Visual Artists and Writers.* New York: Limelight Editions.

RUIZ, DON MIGUEL. 2001. *The Four Agreements: A Practical Guide to Personal Freedom, a Toltec Wisdom Book.* New York: Amber-Allen Publishing.

SMITH, HYRUM W. 1995. *The Ten Natural Laws of Successful Time and Life Management: Proven Strategies for Increased Productivity and Inner Peace.* New York: Warner Books.

STANLEY, THOMAS J., and DANKO, WILLIAM D. 1996. *The Millionaire Next Door: The Surprising Secrets of America's Wealthy.* Atlanta, GA: Longstreet Press.

Resources and Information

Union Offices

Actors' Equity Association (AEA)

New York
165 West 46th St.
New York, NY 10036
Membership, 14th Floor
Reception, 15th Floor
Audition Center, 2nd Floor
(212) 869-8530 (telephone)
(212) 719-9815 (fax)

Orlando (satellite)
10319 Orangewood Blvd.
Orlando, FL 32821
(407) 345-8600 (telephone)
(407) 345-1522 (fax)

Chicago
125 S. Clark Street
Suite 1500
Chicago, IL 60603
(312) 641-0393 (telephone)
(312) 641-6365 (fax)
(312) 641-0418 (audition hotline)

Los Angeles
Museum Square
5757 Wilshire Blvd., Suite One
Los Angeles, CA 90036
(323) 634-1750 (telephone)
(323) 634-1777 (fax)
(323) 634-8980 (pension/health)

San Francisco (satellite)
350 Sansome St., Suite 900
San Francisco, CA 94104
(415) 391-3838 (telephone)
(415) 391-0102 (fax)

Screen Actors Guild (SAG)

New York
360 Madison Avenue, 12th Floor
New York, NY 10017
(212) 944-1030 (main switchboard)
(212) 944-6715 (for deaf performers only: TTY/TTD)

Los Angeles
5757 Wilshire Blvd.
Los Angeles, CA 90036-3600
(323) 954-1600 (main switchboard)
(323) 549-6648 (for deaf performers only: TTY/TTD)
(800) SAG-0767 (for SAG members outside Los Angeles)

American Federation of Television and Radio Artists (AFTRA)

National Office, New York
260 Madison Avenue
New York, NY 10016-2401
(212) 532-0800 (telephone)
(212) 532-2242 (fax)

National Office, Los Angeles
5757 Wilshire Boulevard, 9th Floor
Los Angeles, CA 90036-0800
(323) 634-8100 (telephone)
(323) 634-8194 (fax)

The American Guild of Variety Artists (AGVA)

National Office, New York
184 Fifth Ave., 6th Floor
New York, NY 10010
(212) 675-1003 (telephone)

Trade Publications

Instead of listing all of the possible places you can go on the Internet, I suggest that you go to the Theatre Central page at Playbill.com (www.playbill.com/theatrecentral/sites.html). There you will find most of the information you need. You may wish to search the site for the following links:

- Backstage
- The Ross Reports
- Theatre Communications Group (TCG)
- Variety
- Hollywood Reporter
- TheatreJobs

Generally Useful Websites

Time Management

- Day-Timer: www.daytimer.com
- Day Runner: www.dayrunner.com
- FranklinCovey: www.franklincovey.com
- Stephen Covey's *The Seven Habits of Highly Effective People* book summary: www.quickmba.com/mgmt/7hab/

Financial and Tax Websites

- AnnualCreditReport.com: www.annualcreditreport.com
- Bankrate.com: www.bankrate.com
- Federal Citizen Information Center: www.pueblo.gsa.gov
- The Internal Revenue Service: www.irs.gov
- The Mint (sponsored by Northwestern Mutual): www.themint.org

$\mathcal{B}$iographies

Dan Carbone has been active in San Francisco Bay Area theatre since 1995 as both a playwright and a performer. His solo performance piece *Up from the Ground* won Best of the San Francisco Fringe, an San Francisco Bay Guardian Goldie, and two Upstage/Downstage Awards and was nominated for a Bay Area Theatre Critics' Circle Award for Best Solo Performance. His other plays have included *Salvador Dali Talks to the Animals* (three San Francisco Bay Guardian Upstage/Downstage Awards), *The Pilgrim Project* (Bay Area Theatre Critics' Circle Award for Best Original Script), *There Be Monsters!*, and *Kingdom of Not*.

Debra Cole currently serves as the Actors' Equity Association area liaison for Buffalo and Rochester, New York. She is a founding member of Manhattan Class Company MCC. As an actor, she has performed on Broadway, off Broadway, regionally, and at MCC workshops. Television credits include *Guiding Light*, some A&E and PBS shows, and some commercials. Her company website is www.theseworkingactors.org.

Richard D. Farr is a licensed and registered senior financial advisor with major wire house. Rich earned his MBA and MPS from Cornell University's Johnson Graduate School of Management. He holds the Series 7 General Securities Representative registration and the Series 63 Uniform Securities Agent registration. He is licensed as a life and health insurance agent and holds the Chartered

Retirement Planning Counselor designation and the Certified Financial Manager designation. He has twenty years of experience in financial services focusing on securities portfolio management, interest rate risk management, insurance, and lending. Previously, Rich served as chief financial officer of a multibank holding company, where he specialized in asset and liability management.

Jamie Grady is a professor at Point Park University in Pittsburgh, Pennsylvania, where he teaches in the Sports, Arts, and Entertainment program. Prior to joining academia, Jamie served in a variety of positions for arts organizations throughout the East Coast. Most recently he was a founding member and managing director for the Icarus Theatre Ensemble in Ithaca, New York. He has served as managing director for the Hangar Theatre and for Atlanta's Actor's Express, where he successfully produced *The Harvey Milk Show* as part of the 1996 Cultural Olympiad in conjunction with the 1996 Atlanta Olympic Games. Jamie is a frequent contributor to *ArtsReach* and is the author of *A Simple Statement: A Mission and Vision Approach to Arts Management and Leadership.*

Prudence Heyert is a theater and film actress who may also be seen in commercials directed by such luminaries as M. Night Shyamalan (American Express) and Jim Sheridan (Bayer Aspirin). Upcoming projects include the independent feature film *Neal Cassady* with Tate Donovan and Glenn Fitzgerald and a world premiere production based on the life and times of Leni Riefenstahl where she will play the title role. Prudence has done countless readings, workshops, and independent films around NYC, including *Sitting on the Edge of the World* as part of Manhattan Theatre Source's Playwrighting Development series, *Song of the Shore,* and a staged reading of Dorothy Parker's *Short Stories and Poems* at Mo'Pitkins. Her film *Say That You Love* received the Silver Medal at the Park City Music and Film Festival and was part of the official selection at the Los Angeles International Short Film Festival. An Activist as well as an artist, Prudence was the co-curator of Eve Ensler's VDAY: Until the Violence Stops: Women's Film Festival (2006). Prudence holds a BS in theater from Skidmore College, studied with BADA in London, and graduated from

William Esper Studio's two-year Meisner training program. She currently resides in NYC.

Krista Scott was cofounder and associate director of The New Tradition Theatre Company in St. Cloud, Minnesota, for ten years, where she performed the functions of actor, director, playwright, and educator. She also owned and operated Talent-2-Spare, a non-union talent agency in St. Cloud. She has acted professionally with such companies as Theatre de la Jeune Lune, Hangar Theatre, Kitchen Theatre, Nebraska Repertory, and Nebraska Theatre Caravan and has extensive on-camera and voiceover credits in Minnesota and Nebraska. Other acting credits include the lead roles in *Hedda Gabler* and *Love Letters* in Cairo, Egypt. Her directing credits include *The Bacchae*, *The Laramie Project*, *The Waiting Room*, *Two Rooms*, *The Heidi Chronicles*, *The Glass Menagerie*, *Steel Magnolias*, and *Kiss Me, Kate*, as well as several new play stagings/readings and numerous musical revues. Krista received her MFA in acting from the University of Minnesota and a BFA in acting/directing from Emporia State University. A certified instructor of Fitzmaurice Voicework, she coaches voice and dialects at theatres throughout Central New York and privately, and has held teaching posts at Ithaca College, American University in Cairo, University of Mississippi, Saint Cloud State University, and Concordia College, St. Paul.

Catherine Weidner is an associate professor at DePaul University, teaching classical acting in the BFA and MFA Acting programs. For ten years she was the program director of The Shakespeare Theatre Company Academy for Classical Acting at the George Washington University. Prior to that, she was head of the theatre program for five years at Goddard College in Plainfield, Vermont. She is an actor, teacher, and director. She has worked professionally at The Guthrie Theater and Theatre de la Jeune Lune in Minneapolis, the La Jolla Playhouse in San Diego, and Bread & Puppet in Vermont. She has appeared in *The Heidi Chronicles* by Wendy Wasserstein at Arena Stage; Noel Coward's *Blithe Spirit* and Frederich Schiller's *Mary Stuart* at Center Stage in Baltimore, Maryland; and in *A Streetcar Named Desire* featuring Patricia Clarkson at The Kennedy Center in Washington, DC, directed by

Garry Hynes. In New York, she has directed and performed at the Soho Rep and New Dramatists. In Baltimore, she recently performed in four new plays by James Magruder, *Bad Beans*, at the Baltimore Theatre Project. She had been in staged readings of *Turcaret* by Alain-Rene Lesage at The Shakespeare Theatre Company and *Shakespeare in Hollywood* by Ken Ludwig at The Kennedy Center. She has directed productions of *Richard III*, *Much Ado About Nothing*, *Measure for Measure*, *Waiting for Godot*, *Caligula*, *Otherwise Engaged*, *Animal Farm*, *Reckless*, *Cloud 9*, *The Visit*, and *Ubu*. She also teaches public speaking for the Smithsonian Associates program and works as a private consultant for attorneys, teachers, judges, and other professionals, helping to improve communication, public speaking, and overall clarity in public settings. She has worked with the improvisation troupes Washington Improv Theater and Baltimore Improvisation Group to enhance their performance skills. She is a member of Actors' Equity Association, holds a BFA in acting from Ithaca College and an MFA in directing from the University of Minnesota, and has also trained and performed at The Second City in Chicago and The Neighborhood Playhouse in New York.